I0168000

The
Causeless
Cause

The Eternal Wisdom of
Shwetaashwatara Upanishad

❧

Uttara Nerurkar

The
Causeless
Cause

The Eternal Wisdom of
Shwetaashwatara Upanishad

∾

Uttara Nerurkar

ZEN
PUBLICATIONS
A DIVISION OF MAOLI MEDIA PRIVATE LIMITED

Dedicated to my husband,

Suhas Shripad Nerurkar,

for his unwavering love,

encouragement and support.

The Causeless Cause: The Eternal Wisdom of Shwetaashwatara Upanishad

Copyright © 2016 Uttara Nerurkar

First Edition: November 2016

PUBLISHED BY
ZEN PUBLICATIONS
A Division of Maoli Media Private Limited

60, Juhu Supreme Shopping Centre,
Gulmohar Cross Road No. 9, JVPD Scheme,
Juhu, Mumbai 400 049. India.
Tel: +91 9022208074
eMail: info@zenpublications.com
Website: www.zenpublications.com

COVER & BOOK DESIGN
Red Sky Designs, Mumbai

ISBN 978-93-85902-39-0

All rights reserved. No part of this book may be reproduced or transmitted in any form or by any means, electronic or mechanical, including photocopying, recording, or by any information storage and retrieval system without written permission from the author or her agents, except for the inclusion of brief quotations in a review.

CONTENTS

PREFACE

෨

 This book presumes no prior knowledge whatsoever from the reader of the Vedas, the Upanishads, or, Indian spiritual tenets, in general. In fact, it has originated from the class notes recorded for the students of just such a class taken in 2014 on the little known Shwetaashwatara Upanishad.

It has been written for people who are curious about ancient Indian texts such as the Upanishads but are not familiar with Indian Philosophy in general, and who are therefore unable to understand some aspects of these texts which are critical, but whose explanations are not lucid enough for the first-time reader.

Thus, the explanation of the verses has been reinforced with full explanations of generic concepts of Indian Philosophy, wherever it has been found necessary. At no point will the reader be left wondering what a particular word or statement means. The subject matter itself being very deep, the language has been kept as simple as possible.

I do hope that it will be of help for those who, like me in my previous avatar of a software professional, have little idea of the intricacies of ancient Indian thought and find it difficult to navigate in this unknown territory. I have tried to keep it brief, yet explanatory, with the busy individual in mind. Please do read the Introduction in order to make your foray into this Upanishad smooth!

I wish the reader an exciting journey of discovery!

Uttara Nerurkar
Bangalore

November 15, 2016

Acknowledgements

꩜

First and foremost, I would like to thank the Supreme under whose guidance I have managed to accomplish this work. I am grateful that He considered me a worthy vessel to carry His message. I place this work at His feet.

I am also deeply grateful for the blessings of my parents, Shri Vinod Chandra Gupta and Shrimati Usha Gupta, who have always guided me toward the right path.

This book is inspired by my student, Divya Krishnan, who, after studying the class notes for the Upanishad, exclaimed that it would be so wonderful if people outside our classroom could also have access to this concise and lucid commentary. Once I did take up the pen, she became the first editor of my manuscript, and dutifully corrected my errors, particularly those hidden in the Sanskrit verses, and gave valuable inputs on the content.

The book was also the result of enquiries from the readers of my monthly column in Dayanand Sandesh, who wanted to know whether I had written books that they could purchase. Chief among these was Shri Mahavir ji, ex-Vice Chancellor of Gurukul Kangri Vishwavidyalaya, who told me that it was high time that I wrote one. I was overwhelmed by this, and finally got down to penning the little that I had learnt during the course of my studies, teaching and practice.

Serendipitously, I chanced upon my friend, Mrunalini Katiyar, a professional editor, as the book was taking its final shape. She happily took up the work of editing my work as a professional. I am really grateful to her for all her assistance in not only editing the book, but also being my pro bono agent with the publishers.

I thank the publishers, Zen Publications, for giving me a platform to present my ideas to the world. Their professionalism was remarkable, and they made the process extremely smooth.

I gratefully acknowledge the inputs I have received during my class from all my students. Not only did they add value to the class, but I have modified my commentary based on their discussions and feedback.

I would be remiss in my duties if I did not mention my sister, Rajyashree Agarwala, for her constant encouragement; and my brother, Samudra Gupta, as also my friend, Rachna Dheer, who helped me with pointers for publication.

Last, but surely not the least, I lovingly thank my husband, Suhas Shripad Nerurkar, for always being there for me, and assisting me in every imaginable way.

I hope my readers will enjoy this work and will send me their feedback.

Om Shriparamaatmane namaH!

INTRODUCTION

*U*panishads lie at the very core of ancient Indian spiritual thought. They are highly revered by Indians and the rest of the world alike. They contain answers to the deepest mystical questions that have troubled man since the beginning of time. They delve into the mystery of the nature of this Universe, its purpose, the entities that inhabit it, the relationship between them and the ultimate goal of life. Due to this esoteric subject matter, they are considered Upaangas, or a subordinate part, of the Vedas – the supreme revered books of the Hindus. Some even call them 'the essence of the Vedas', though this epithet may not be entirely justified.

Their antiquity can only be guessed as it lies in the hoary past. Of the 200-odd Upanishads that are available today, ten Upanishads are considered the most authoritative. They are called the ten principal Upanishads. These include Isha, Kena, Katha, Prashna, Mundaka, Maandookya, Taittareeya, Aitreya, Chhandogya and Brihadaaranyaka, laid down in this mnemonic verse –

ईशकेनकठप्रश्न – मुण्डमाण्डूक्यतित्तिरि ।
ऐतरेयं च छान्दोग्यं बृहदारण्यकं तथा ॥

Shwetaashwatara Upanishad is not one of them. However, it is considered the eleventh due to its importance and clear exposition of spiritual matters. It is also an apt Upanishad for beginners as, firstly, it uses direct language and is not as symbolic as the other Upanishads; and secondly, because it has a lot of Vaidika verses borrowed in toto. This gives a useful introduction to some of the most beautiful Vaidika verses.

The Upanishad is divided into six chapters, with 113 verses in all (16, 17, 21, 22, 14, 23, respectively). The metres of the verses are typically Trishtup and, in a few cases, Anushtup. These are very popular metres in Sanskrit works. Other metres occur in only a handful of verses.

Understanding the following basic concepts of Indian spiritual thought, which are themselves in line with Vaidika precepts, will be very helpful for beginners.

1. There are three eternal entities in this Universe –

    a. Inanimate matter, **Prakrti,** which has a base primordial form at the beginning of the Universe that transforms to yield the whole multipicity of objects we see around us. These transformations are transient, and return to their basic form upon complete destruction.

    b. Individual souls, **Jeevaatmaas,** that reside in each living being and are animate.

    c. The one Supreme Soul, **Paramaatmaa,** or God, who is animate and is the creator, controller and destroyer of the Universe.

2. The Universe comes into existence as **Srishti,** expands and diversifies over the period of creation, or **Kalpa**. It ends in **Pralaya** when everything is reduced to its primordial form. This lasts as long as the Kalpa. The whole period of a Kalpa and Pralaya comprises a 'Day of Brahma'. The cycle repeats itself ad infinitum. Like a rotating wheel, it has no beginning or end to it. This may be termed a 'cyclical infinity'.

3. The material body is the abode of the soul. When the body

encompassing a soul dies, the soul continues to exist. It moves on to another body made of matter in an eternal cycle of birth, death and re-incarnation. God never occupies a body.

4. Living beings are born as different species, in a hierarchy starting from the plant world, moving on to viruses, bacteria, insects, fishes, amphibians, lower animals and mammals, with man at the top of the pyramid. Human birth is considered the pinnacle, as it has the most discerning intellect and the maximum capacity for well-thought-out action vis-à-vis instinctive behaviour. It also has the maximum capacity for enjoyment of the material world. The soul, particularly in the human birth, is independent in performing its actions.

5. This structure is not unjust. It is based upon the deeds that a soul performs. Actions lead to equal reactions (as opposed to Newton's Third Law which states that action and reaction are equal and opposite!). Thus, a benevolent deed results in happiness; a sinful deed leads to sorrow. Some deeds affect the soul's happiness in this birth; others come to fruition in future births. This is the **Law of Action (Karma).**

6. While the cycle of life and death continues endlessly, it is possible for a soul to exit the cycle by means of salvation, or **Moksha**. This is a non-obvious path that cannot be reasoned out by any available data. Therefore, it forms the subject matter of all the Upanishads in particular, and other spiritual texts in general. They are based on the experiences of enlightened sages, such as Sage Shwetaashwatara himself. The Upanishad under consideration here has been written by his disciples, as is evident from a verse towards the end of the text.

7. In Philosophy, a 'cause' does not always refer to a reason. In fact, it usually refers to something that leads to a change, called an 'effect'. For example, milk transforms into butter. Then, milk is the cause of butter, and butter is the effect of milk. Anything which leads to the transformation of milk to butter is its cause, too.

There are three types of causes identified in Indian Philosophy – the efficient cause (Nimitta Kaarana), the material cause (Upaadaana Kaarana) and the general cause (Saamaanya Kaarana). These can be understood by the time-tested example of a potter making an earthen pot on his wheel. The potter is the efficient cause of the pot, who provides the motivation, the volition and the effort in producing the pot. Without him, the process would not start, nor would it have any direction. The clay provides the material that goes into the pot; hence, it is called the material cause. All the other instruments used by the potter, like the wheel and the stick, are general causes. Time and space are the over-arching general causes for all effects.

EXPLANATORY NOTE ON THE VAIDIKA WORDS

Vaidika words are not fixed in their meaning. They are derived from a root and a combination of prefixes and suffixes. Each of these components has one or more meanings, and influences the meaning of the final word. Thus, the final word itself can have many meanings. Which meaning is applicable at a particular location is determined based on the context, and is left to the experts in the field to decide. We see this on a much smaller scale in our everyday language, like the word 'well', that could mean a repository of water, or health, or goodness, or just an interjection.

In the same manner, the word 'Brahma', which is used very often in the Upanishads, including the Shwetaashwatara Upanishad, has several meanings depending on the context. Typically, it means the Supreme, i.e., God, but it could have many other meanings as well. Arising from the root 'Brh' meaning 'to be large' or 'to expand or 'to make a sound', the word can typically have the following meanings –

- Huge

- The Supreme because He is huge – larger than the Universe, in fact!

- The Universe, also called Brahmaanda, because it is huge

- The Vedas because they transmit the knowledge of large things – the Supreme, the Universe and life, in general

- The Braahmana, i.e., the knower of the Vedas and/or the Supreme

- The Jeevaatmaa because it is much greater than inanimate matter.

There are some more words that will be found to have several meanings, sometimes in the same verse, leading to several meanings of the verse itself! I have tried to cover these alternative meanings in my commentary .

In the Vedas, God occurs in all three genders – masculine, feminine and neuter. Sometimes multiple genders are found in the same verse! I have tried to translate the Sanskrit verse truthfully with the gender as given. This makes for some awkward reading in English at times, but I think the readers will appreciate the closeness of the translation to the original. Also, I have tried to make up for it in the ensuing explanation.

Explanatory Notes on This Commentary

1. The first paragraph of the commentary following a verse is as close to a literal translation of the verse as possible and is in italics. Brackets are generally used to indicate the 'unsaid' in the verse; rarely, in the interests of readability, have they been done away with.

2. The next paragraph(s), if present, contains a detailed explanation of the verse to fully understand its purport.

3. The word 'Soul' always refers to the individual soul, or Jeevaatmaa, and never to Paramaatmaa. Also, the word 'Consciousness', when used as a noun, denotes the soul.

4. Sanskrit words have been capitalised. Instead of diacritical

marks to denote their correct pronunciation, devices such as 'aa' to represent ā, 'ee' for ī, etc., have been used to simplify the reading experience.

5. Some English words have also been capitalised in order to emphasise their unique usage. For example, 'Matter' is used to denote 'the physical substance, the thing that objects are made up of', and the capital M distinguishes it from its other meanings, viz., subject or problem.

6. In general, words in the male gender include the female gender and vice versa.

❧

CHAPTER ONE

The Cause of the Universe

∿

The Upanishad begins with an enquiry into the possible cause, or causes, of the Universe. It then immediately plunges into answering that question in this – the very first chapter. It also explains in brief the nature of the Universe, the place of beings in it and the way for them to attain salvation.

ब्रह्मवादिनो वदन्ति –
किं कारणं ब्रह्म कुतः स्म जाता
जीवाम केन क्व च सम्प्रतिष्ठाः ।
अधिष्ठिताः केन सुखेतरेषु
वर्तामहे ब्रह्मविदो व्यवस्थाम् ॥ १। १॥

The scholars discussing Brahma say, "O knowers of Brahma! What is this cause that is Brahma? From where have we originated? To what do we owe our lives? Where is our support? Who is supervising this order we exist in (in the Universe that we observe), consisting of happiness and sorrow?

It is clear that there is an order to everything in this Universe. Therefore, it is logical to presume that happiness and sorrow are also following someone's or something's bidding and are not entirely random.

In this way, the Upanishad sets the stage for its subject matter, bringing into sharp focus the highly elevated thinking of the Vaidika seers.

In this verse, Brahma implies large.[1] So, the verse inquires – What is the large cause of this large Universe? The Universe being large, and its order being maintained perfectly at every instant and at every point, its cause must be present everywhere. This implies that it must be at least the same size as the Brahmaanda, or Universe, if not larger than it.[2]

The scholars start by eliminating the causes that seem most obvious. They say –

कालः स्वभावो नियतिर्यदृच्छा
भूतानि योनिः पुरुष इति चिन्त्या ।
संयोग एषां न त्वात्मभावा-
दात्माप्यनीशः सुखदुःखहेतोः ॥ १।२॥

It is worth considering by Man whether Time, the nature of things, a prescribed order, happenstance or Matter itself is the cause (of the Universe and its order). (However) even the combination (of one or more of these) does not explain the existence of Consciousness. Also, even the Soul is subservient in the matter of experiencing happiness or sorrow (if it was not, it would always opt for happiness, and nobody would be unhappy).

A number of processes have Time as one of their causes, if not the sole cause, e.g., aging, the healing of wounds. It is the nature of some things to cause some events, e.g., the gravitational pull of the Sun makes the Earth go round it, fire will always burn substances brought in contact with it. Some things happen due to a well-defined

---

1 See explanatory note in the Introduction.

2 Usually, Brahma is interpreted as God in this verse, which is the word's usual meaning. However, if God is already known as the cause, the other questions in the verse are automatically answered. Nor is the discussion in the next few verses necessary. So, this meaning does not really apply here.

order, e.g., a seed sprouts only when water and air are present. Some things seem to happen accidentally, e.g., the current theory about why the Big Bang did not lead to a perfectly uniform Universe relies on an aberration occurring 'accidentally'. Matter may be considered the cause for creating the Universe the way it is by its very nature, as it does in the case of river valleys and canyons. However, as per ancient Indian philosophy, inanimate matter could never create consciousness. Therefore, all these causes could explain some limited phenomena, but they do not explain the whole Universe. Similarly, the Soul itself is found to be subservient to a higher order in the dispensation of happiness and sorrow. So, it could not be the cause, either.

Having eliminated all the causes that are available to direct perception –

ते ध्यानयोगानुगता अपश्यन्
देवात्मशक्तिं स्वगुणैर्निगूढाम् ।
यः कारणानि निखिलानि तानि
कालात्मयुक्तान्यधितिष्ठत्येकः ॥ १।३ ॥

The seers went into deep meditation and observed a Divine Force that was concealed by its very properties. They discovered that this One presided over all the causes from Time to the Soul.

This implies that the other causes mentioned in the previous verse are causes in their own right, but are limited in their effect. Since together they create this precisely functioning Creation, there must be a single entity, viz., God, who is operating behind all of them.

The deeper implication is that God cannot be surmised by studying Nature alone. Today, we find that physicists and astronomers believe that everything can be explained through equations, through the nature of Matter – no external entity needs to be surmised. It is the ones studying biology or medicine who can see inexplicable forces at work!

Before embarking on describing this One, the Upanishatkaara (the author of the Upanishad) wants to get the discussion regarding Matter out of the way. It may seem that a discussion on inanimate Matter is out-of-context in an Upanishad, but most Upanishads cover this aspect, as it is impossible to discuss what to get into without mentioning what to get out of! So, the seer starts describing the Universe –

तमेकनेमिं त्रिवृतं षोडशान्तं
शतार्धारं विंशतिप्रत्यराभिः ।
अष्टकैः षड्भिर्विश्वरूपैकपाशं
त्रिमार्गभेदं द्विनिमित्तैकमोहम् ॥ १ । ४ ॥

The Universe is like a wheel, which has one felly (made of primordial Matter that circumscribes the wheel). This felly has three layers (made of the three properties of Matter – Sattva, Raja and Tama). It is sixteen-pointed, (the points/ends being the visible elementary gross products, consisting of the five elements, the five senses of perception, the five organs of action [arms, legs, speech, excretory and reproductive organs] and the mind).[3] It has 50 spokes holding the wheel up, (representing the 50 types of mental states of a being).[4] There are 20 counterspokes, (which represent subdivisions of the mental states). There are six groups of eight (that are not well understood). There is one snare or net extending across the Universe. There are three roads (for the wheel – the one that leads to salvation [Devayaanam], the one that leads to human birth [Pitryaanam] and the one that leads to other lower forms of life [Tiryak Yoni]). The road is determined by two causes (good and evil deeds). (At the very centre of the wheel lies) the

---

3 *Alternatively, this could be the sixteen Kalaas – life-breath (Praana), belief (Shraddhaa), the five elements, the five senses (counted as one unit), the mind, food (Anna), reproductive power (Veerya), Austerity (Tapa), knowledge (Mantra), deeds (Karma), residences (Loka) and language (Naama), but then the five elements, five senses and the mind would be repeated. That is why this explanation may not hold water.*

4 *The fifty mental states consist of 5 types of ignorance (Ajnaana), 28 types of disability (Ashakti), 9 types of satisfaction (Tushti), 8 types of achievement (Siddhi).*

one (root-cause of) delusion (i.e., the belief that the Soul is the Body).

This verse represents the Universe as a wheel. This is a very potent metaphor because it paints the image of something that keeps rolling with no beginning and no end. We cannot say when was the first Creation and when will be the last, because there is no such thing as the first or the last Creation, just like in a line which extends infinitely in the positive and negative direction, there is no meaning of the first or the last point from any point in its middle. This is a concept which no ancient civilization other than the Indian can boast to have mooted!

Also, it should be noted that the Universe is seen as a single net, where everything is interconnected. The action of one being causes repercussions all over the Universe! This one is a relatively new idea in modern science.

The meaning of some of the sets mentioned has been lost over time.

The next verse is about the Body-Soul combination. Again, the meanings of the sets mentioned in the verse should be taken with a pinch of salt, as their true meaning seems to be lost in time. The Brahmavaadis say –

पञ्चस्रोतोऽम्बुं पञ्चयोन्युग्रवक्रां
पञ्चप्राणोर्मि पञ्चबुद्ध्यादिमूलम् ।
पञ्चावर्तां पञ्चदुःखौघवेगां
पञ्चाशद्भेदां पञ्चपर्वामधीमः ॥ १।५॥

We study (the Body,[5] which is like a river that) has five streams of water (the five senses), five sources (of subtle matter, the Pancha Tanmaatraas) which are very aggressive and twisted, five waves of the life-breath (Praana), one basis (the mind) which registers five

5 *The subject of the verse is not explicitly mentioned in the verse. All commentators have called it the Universe, but, by the commonly agreed meaning of the verse, this is obviously not so. Therefore, I have taken the meaning of Body rather than the Universe.*

types of signals from the senses, five whirlpools (of the objects of the senses, that suck us into worldly pleasures), five rapids of sorrow (sorrows encountered in the womb, birth, old age, disease and death), 50 branches (of mental states as described in the previous verse) and five sections (five Kleshas = Avidyaa, Asmitaa, Raaga, Dwesha and Abhinivesha).

The Praanas are divided into five –

    1. Praana – Exhaled breath

    2. Apaana – Inhaled breath

    3. Vyaana – that which causes movement in the body

    4. Samaana – that which spreads the digested contents to the body

    5. Udaana – that which controls peristaltic motion

The Kleshas are defined by Patanjali in Yogadarshanam as follows –

    1. Avidyaa is the ignorance about the reality of things.

    2. Asmitaa is the misplaced belief that the body is the same as the Soul.

    3. Raaga is the attraction to other beings, or to worldly objects.

    4. Dwesha is repulsion from the same.

    5. Abhinivesha is the fear of death.

All these are actually forms of Avidyaa itself, as can be readily seen.

The verse thus describes the River of Life representing the condition of each and every being, particularly the human being, in the Universe.

सर्वाजीवे सर्वसंस्थे बृहन्ते
अस्मिन् हंसो भ्राम्यते ब्रह्मचक्रे ।
पृथगात्मानं प्रेरितारं च मत्वा
जुष्टस्ततस्तेनामृतत्वमेति ॥ १ । ६॥

The Hansa (Soul) is moved around in this gigantic Wheel of the Universe, which gives it life and support. However, when it figures out that there is a difference between itself and the Mover of the Universe, it attains salvation by the grace of the latter.

In common Sanskrit, Hansa refers to the swan, but the generic meaning is not restricted to that. The word derives from the root 'Han' meaning 'to destroy/harm' or 'to move'. Here, the latter meaning is applicable in the case of the individual soul that moves from body to body.

Expanding further on the last verse, the seer exults –

उद्गीतमेतत् परमं तु ब्रह्म
तस्मिंस्त्रयं सुप्रतिष्ठाक्षरं च ।
अत्रान्तरं ब्रह्मविदो विदित्वा
लीना ब्रह्मणि तत्परा योनिमुक्ताः ॥ १।७॥

This Supreme Brahma (as mentioned in the previous verse) is the One sung about by the Vedas. In it is located the triad (the three Lokas of the stellar regions [Dyuloka], the non-luminous regions [Prthiveeloka] and the intervening space [Antariksha] – in short, the whole Universe). It is the greatest support of the Universe and is imperishable. In this world, the knowers of Brahma, seeing It as inside everything, devote themselves to It. Immersed in Brahma, their Souls are released from embodiment.

संयुक्तमेतत् क्षरमक्षरं च
व्यक्ताव्यक्तं भरते विश्वमीशः ।
अनीशश्चात्मा बध्यते भोक्तृभावाज्-
ज्ञात्वा देवं मुच्यते सर्वपाशैः ॥ १।८॥

The Lord conjoins the perishable (Matter) with the imperishable (Soul), the visible (Matter) with the invisible (Soul) (in the body of the living being), and (then) supports the combination. The subservient

Soul is trapped due to its desire to consume (forms of Matter), but, when it comes to know that Divine One, it is released from all the snares (of life, i.e., the being attains salvation).

Till the time that the Soul is immersed in the pleasures of this world, reincarnation is inevitable. The non-obvious path is that of aligning with God and giving up this world. This alone can spare him the sorrows of birth, living and death.

This next verse describes beautifully and succinctly the three entities that make up the Universe and their relationship with each other –

ज्ञाज्ञौ द्वावजावीशनीशा-
वजा ह्येका भोक्तृभोग्यार्थयुक्ता ।
अनन्तश्चात्मा विश्वरूपो ह्यकर्ता
लयं यदा विन्दते ब्रह्मेतत् ॥ १।९ ॥

There are two unborn ones – One who knows (everything) and the one who doesn't (i.e., knows little, as opposed to nothing at all); One who is the Lord of all, and the other who is subservient. Then, there is one unborn female (Primordial Matter), which is deployed to provide for the consumption of the consumer (Soul). The Soul has no end (in Time, not Space); it attains all kinds of forms (by moving from body to body); it is a non-doer (while it seems to be doing all the deeds, it is actually Matter that is making it do so). When it understands this triad, it achieves this Brahma (the Lord).[6]

6 *The commentators have unequivocally considered Brahma to be the One who has the attributes of the third line in the verse. Interpreted thus, the meaning of the third and fourth lines becomes – God is limitless (in Space and Time), is represented by all the forms in the Universe and, even though It is the Creator, Preserver and Destroyer, really performs no action, as the deeds are 'Nishkaama Karma' - without any motive for Himself. When the Sou witnesses this trinity of Matter, Self and Brahma, it then attains Brahma.*
However, interpreted this way, the subject 'Atmaa' is not available to the verb 'Vindate', as it has been used for Brahma in the third line. The words 'the Soul' then have to be assumed to complete the meaning of the fourth line. This is because of the insistence that the Soul is the doer. That the Soul is the Kartaa is true at the gross level. However, in the ultimate analysis, this is not so. Even the Bhagwad-gita says – कार्यकारणकर्तृत्वे हेतुः प्रकृतिरुच्यते। पुरुषः सुखदुःखानां भोक्तृत्वे हेतुरुच्यते ॥१३।२०॥ - i.e., Nature is called the cause of the causes and the effects (of matter in this Universe), and of doer-ship, while the soul is said to be the consumer of happiness and sorrow. This is a very subtle subject, and can be passed over in the first reading.

In this verse, there is a play on the word 'Aja' which has two meanings – 'the unborn' and 'the goat'. The metaphor of the goat helps us to remember the verse. However, the real meaning intended is 'unborn' to indicate that all these three entities are never created, and hence are without an end, i.e., all three are eternal.

For a spiritual seeker, it is very important to understand the three eternal entities in this Universe – Matter, Souls and God. We have a tendency to equate ourselves with our body. Without knowing the characteristics of Matter, and those of the completely different Soul, it is not possible to ever be free of that misunderstanding. Brahma is particularly difficult to reason out, as It is nowhere to be found! Even the seers have to go into meditation to find it. Scriptures, like this one, introduce us to this knowledge.

Clarifying the adjectives in the previous verse, so that no doubt remains, the seer explains –

क्षरं प्रधानममृताक्षरं हरः

क्षरात्मानावीशते देव एकः ।

तस्याभिध्यानाद्योजनात् तत्त्वभावाद्

भूयश्चान्ते विश्वमायानिवृत्तिः ॥ १ । १० ॥

The perishable one is Matter, the imperishable one is the undying Hara (meaning 'the one that travels from one birth to another', i.e., the Soul). The One Divinity rules over both of them – perishable Matter and the Soul.[7] *By meditating upon It, by connecting to Its reality/ essence/true form again and again, in the end, all Maayaa (delusion) is rid (from the Soul).*

The word 'Vishva', particularly in ancient texts, hardly ever means 'the world' because the Sanskrit word actually means 'all'. We saw this in the last verse, too, in the word 'Vishvaroopa'.

'Maayaa' has become a buzzword and now is an entity by itself!

---

[7] *Note here that the word 'Atmaa' is again used here to denote the Soul rather than God, as in the previous verse.*

However, in ancient texts, it simply refers to the delusion that the Soul is the body it occupies. Or, even the delusion that there is no such thing as Brahma! Connecting with Brahma through Dhyaana is the only way to reach Him. As the Yajurveda exhorts –

तमेव विदित्वातिमृत्युमेति नान्यः पन्था विद्यतेऽयनाय ॥यजु०३१।१८॥

– *Knowing Him alone, one transcends death; there is no other path for salvation.*

The result of seeing God is detailed thus –

ज्ञात्वा देवं सर्वपाशापहानिः
क्षीणैः क्लेशैर्जन्ममृत्युप्रहाणिः ।
तस्याभिध्यानात् तृतीयं देहभेदे
विश्वैश्वर्यं केवल आप्तकामः ॥ १।११॥

Knowing the Divine, (the Soul is) rid of all the snares (trapping it in this world). By the destruction of the sorrows (Kleshas),[8] the Cycle of Birth and Death is broken. By meditating on It regularly, (the Soul attains) the Third (i.e., the Supreme),[9] and on the separation from the body (death), it attains lordship over everything, comes into its own and achieves the fulfilment of all its desires.

Thus, again, the *only* route to salvation is by knowing, or realising, the Divine One.

Kevala is a very loaded word in the scriptures. As used in everyday language, it means 'alone' or 'only'. Thus, God is Kevala because It is always unattached to anything else. The Soul is usually attached to Matter, leading to happiness and sorrow. When it is rid of this encumbrance, it also becomes Kevala – alone and, hence, blissful.

I always had difficulty in understanding Aaptakaama (the one whose every desire is fulfilled), because first we were being asked to get rid of all our desires, and when we had no desires left, the

8 See verse 1|5 for explanation.
9 'The third' is taken to mean 'the third loka', i.e., Heaven (Swargaloka). However, by context and as given in the ninth verse, we are talking of the third entity. The 'third' is, thus, already defined by the previous verse.

seers said, "All your desires will be fulfilled." This made no sense whatsoever! And no explanation was forthcoming in any text that I could lay my hands on. Over time, I have come to realise that the last remaining desire of the sages is to be rid of material encumbrances and to obtain a glimpse of, first, themselves, and then, their beloved – Brahma. *This* is what is attained by the Aaptakaamas! Having fulfilled their last and toughest desire, they are finally devoid of any yearning...

एतज्ज्ञेयं नित्यमेवात्मसंस्थं
नातः परं वेदितव्यं हि किञ्चित् ।
भोक्ता भोग्यं प्रेरितारं च मत्वा
सर्वं प्रोक्तं त्रिविधं ब्रह्ममेतत् ॥१।१२॥

One should know this (Lord) who always resides in one's soul. There is nothing to be known beyond It. Knowing the consumer, the consumed and the Motivator, all is said about this threefold Brahma (the Universe, which is composed of these three only). [10]

The means for attaining the Supreme and an understanding of His presence are described in this verse –

वह्नेर्यथा योनिगतस्य मूर्तिर्-
न दृश्यते नैव च लिङ्गनाशः ।
स भूय एवेन्धनयोनिगृह्यस्-
तद्वोभयं वै प्रणवेन देहे ॥१।१३॥

The form of the fire that is located in its source – e.g., the firewood – is not seen. However, its sign is not destroyed (as) it can be obtained again and again by rubbing together the upper piece of wood (Indhana)

---

10 *Commentators typically translate the Brahma here as God and the meaning is given as "All is thus said about this threefold Brahma", implying that all three – the consumer, the consumed and the Motivator are but one. This goes against the spirit of the verse, and the previous and following verse, i.e., the context. Also, it goes against the spirit of not only this verse, but verse after verse, nay, the Upanishad itself, where the difference between the consumer, the consumed and the Motivator is delineated again to again to ensure that the seeker is left under no illusion.*

and the lower piece of wood (Yoni). In the same way, in this body (made of Matter that is consumed), the two (the consumer and the Motivator – from the previous verse) can be obtained by means of Pranava (the sound of Om).

How exactly this is to be done is described in the next verse –

स्वदेहमरणिं कृत्वा प्रणवं चोत्तरारणिम् ।
ध्याननिर्मथनाभ्यासाद्देवं पश्येन्निगूढवत् ॥ १ । १४ ॥

Make your body the lower piece of wood, and Om the upper piece of wood. By rubbing the two together repeatedly in deep meditation (i.e., use your body to focus and meditate repeatedly on Om), you will see the Divine, as if He was hidden.

Just like fire was hidden in the pieces of the wood and needed some effort to take it out, the seer has no reason to doubt the presence of God, as signs of Him are available all around her. With this unswerving faith, she sets about searching deep in her soul. God is not situated in some location, be it some body of water or a statue made of stone. He is situated everywhere. However, the location He makes Himself apparent to the yearning Soul is within that Soul itself!

For the practice of Om Japa, one should make oneself still and repeat and mull over Om in one's mind, thinking of God's various properties. These properties are not that of the dress that a statue wears in a particular temple, or its jewellery, but they are the ones that are truly God's alone, like the ones mentioned in the earlier verses and those to follow.

Continuing the metaphors from the previous verses, the seer says –

तिलेषु तैलं दधनीव सर्पि-
रापः स्रोतःस्वरणीषु चाग्निः ।

एवमात्मात्मनि गृह्यतेऽसौ
सत्येनैनं तपसा योऽनुपश्यति ॥ १।१५॥

Just as oil is obtained from (crushed) sesame seeds, butter is obtained from curd (on churning), waters are obtained from their sources and fire is obtained from wood, so also, the Supreme is obtained inside one's Soul by one who sees Him through the practice of truthfulness and self-control.

In the four examples mentioned, that which is derived is not obviously present to the naked eye. However, the intelligent person knows how to extract the product from its source. Similar is the case with God. For the one who wishes to see God, truthfulness and the desire to ferret it out has to be over-arching.

Today, we are told that this is also true and its opposite is also true, or that nothing is the truth, everything is relative and a shade of grey. This is a falsity. **The truth is always one.** You may know it or you may not; you may be in a position to know it or you may not. That does not make the truth different, it does not make the truth 'grey'. You may have come to believe that there is no single truth and that it varies with people's perspectives. But, if you think deeply, you will realise that the perspective may differ, but the truth does not. Just as different people may see yellow as yellow or orange, but that does not change the frequency of the radiation, which stays unique.

If you *do* wish to know the real thing, the path is straight and narrow, ridden with great temptations and difficulties on all sides. That is why the seer is often called 'Dheera' – the steadfast one. Remaining steadfast on one's quest, ignoring all the various forks that seem to lead in the same direction but are oh! so much easier, is fortitude, or Tapa.

Emphasising, as it were, the previous verse, the seer says –

सर्वव्यापिनमात्मानं क्षीरे सर्पिरिवार्पितम् ।
आत्मविद्यातपोमूलं तद्ब्रह्मोपनिषत् परम् ॥
तद्ब्रह्मोपनिषत् परम् ॥ १।१६॥

That Omnipresent (Supreme) Soul is present in everything, just as butter is present in (every drop of) milk. He lies at the root of (i.e., is attained by) knowledge of oneself and the Supreme (Aatmavidyaa), and by austerity (Tapa). This teaching regarding Brahma is the ultimate sermon.

Once the devotee has single-mindedly sought truth and ensured that bodily pleasures do not sway him from that path, he observes God in everything around him, like butter in milk.

The last two words are repeated by tradition to indicate the end of the chapter.

CHAPTER TWO

Attaining Salvation

∾

Having established the cause of the Universe, the components making it up, their nature and their relationship to each other, the seer now focusses on the main subject matter of the Upanishad – how to attain God. The context is set by reiterating the first five verses from Yajurveda, Chapter 11. These verses talk about meditation, and form part of the Upaasanaa Kaanda (meditation section) of the Vedas.

The first verse gives an overall guideline for enlightenment –

युञ्जानः प्रथमं मनस्तत्त्वाय सविता धियः ।
अग्नेर्ज्योतिर्निचाय्य पृथिव्या अध्याभरत् ॥२।१॥

For true knowledge, the motivated seeker should connect/yoke his mind to his intellect. (This unswerving meditation, or Samaadhi, will lead him to the light/knowledge of Agni - the Supreme.) Extracting the light from that Agni, he should spread it throughout his body, or among other human beings (both meanings being valid).

As per Indian Philosophy, the mind is composed of four parts. These are –

1. Mana – or, loosely, the mind, which receives signals from the senses, filters out one and forwards it to the Buddhi. Also, it receives commands from the Buddhi to execute movements of the body. Mana may be understood as the input/output processor of the Body-computer.

2. Buddhi – or the intellect, that analyses the information coming from the Mana, accesses the database in the memory (Chitta), and makes sense of the incoming information. It commands the Mana to take appropriate bodily action. It is also the logic or thought centre. It may be likened to the CPU of a computer.

3. Chitta – this is the memory store, like the hard drive of a computer, and provides access for storage and retrieval of memories.

4. Ahankaara – loosely, the ego. It makes the Soul identify with the Body.

The mantra exhorts the seeker to dissolve the movements of his Mana into his Buddhi, and thence into the Supreme. That is when he will discover the light (Agni) of the Lord. He should then spread the knowledge of God into every part of his material body as it were, so that his Ahankaara is completely shed. Also, he should not restrict this knowledge to himself, but should spread it among other seekers, so that their path becomes easier.

This next mantra continues the thought and exhorts the seeker to put in great effort to attain Samaadhi –

युक्तेन मनसा वयं देवस्य सवितुः सवे । सुवर्गेयाय शक्त्या ॥ २ । २ ॥[1]

For the attainment of heavenly bliss, we connect our mind to the glory of the Divine Creator of the world (in deep Samaadhi) with all our strength.

---

1 *The Upanishad contains a slightly distorted version of the Vaidika verse, which runs as follows –* युक्तेन मनसा वयं देवस्य सवितुः सवे । स्वर्ग्याय शक्त्या ॥यजुर्वेद १ १ । २ ॥

Meditation to control the mind requires great and sustained effort, but the rewards far outweigh that effort.

The next verse extols the results of meditation –

युक्त्वाय मनसा देवान् सुवर्यतो धिया दिवम् ।
बृहज्ज्योतिः करिष्यतः सविता प्रसुवाति तान् ॥ २। ३ ॥[2]

On controlling the senses through the mind, and knowledge through the intellect, the Supreme Motivator and Creator responds by creating great light and knowledge in the intellect, that, in turn, pleases the senses, the mind and the intellect (i.e., He gives great happiness to the Soul and a pure, healthy body and mind).

Those who meditate on God not only find what they seek, but before that they are blessed with a lot of knowledge in the form of revelations. This makes them ready for the ultimate revelation of God Himself.

The next verse describes the path in more detail –

युञ्जते मन उत युञ्जते धियो
विप्रा विप्रस्य बृहतो विपश्चितः ।
वि होत्रा दधे वयुनाविदेक
इन्मही देवस्य सवितुः परिष्टुतिः ॥ २। ४ ॥

Just like the most learned of seers had merged their minds and their intellects in the great eulogy of the Most Knowledgeable, the Greatest, the All-Seer, the Creator and the Divine in deep meditation, so also I, desirous of finding Him, and so having eagerly absorbed all knowledge (from them), sit alone in meditation.

Knowledge is the first step in seeking God. If we have not

---

2 *The Vaidika verse here reads as follows -*
युक्त्वाय सविता देवान्त्स्वर्यतो धिया दिवम् । बृहज्ज्योतिः करिष्यतः सविता प्रसुवाति तान् ॥यजुर्वेद ११।३॥

understood what is Dharma and what are the secrets of the Universe, of Life itself, we cannot hope to be graced by God's presence.

Seclusion and renunciation are the next most important in the path of God. The Ultimate cannot be achieved without the ultimate sacrifice. Just as two lovers give up their 'zone of comfort' – their established lifestyles and relationships – in order to start a new life together, so too it is with the Soul and the Supreme.

This mantra asks the seeker to find the right Guru, as this is crucial in the discovery of God –

युजे वां ब्रह्म पूर्व्यं नमोभिर्-
वि श्लोक एतु पथ्येव सूरेः ।
शृण्वन्तु विश्वे अमृतस्य पुत्रा
आ ये धामानि दिव्यानि तस्थुः ॥ २।५॥

I connect with you two – the Guru who has already seen Brahma, and with Brahma – with deep respect. May the fame of the enlightened ones spread far and wide like a path (leads to a destination, i.e., may teacher's fame lead me to him and may his teaching enlighten me, too)! O listen everyone to the true children of the Undying Supreme, the sons who are situated in regions of divine light (i.e., those who have seen God and are experiencing his brilliance)!

In the final lap to Brahma, it is important to find somebody who has already seen Him, as he alone can take the seeker all the way. The verse prays for being able to find such a Yogi. The seeker also pleads to these Yogis, who are sitting on the verge of attaining Moksha, to hear his call. The mantra also makes a plea that these great seers should not go unheard – everyone should follow the path they illuminate.

From the next verse till verse 2|15, the seer Shwetaashwatara elaborates on the above five Vaidika verses. The first verse draws a parallel between the sacred fire-sacrifice (Yajna) and the process of enlightenment –

अग्निर्यत्राभिमथ्यते वायुर्यत्राधिरुध्यते ।
सोमो यत्रातिरिच्यते तत्र संजायते मनः ॥२।६॥

Where the fire is kindled through rubbing (two pieces of wood at the start of the yajna), where the air is halted (at the sacrificial altar, as if in anticipation of the sacrifice), where the juice of the medicinal herb Soma is extracted (as is often done in a yajna), there arises the Mind.

This Yajna metaphor of Samaadhi translates to: Where the Japa of Om is done as per 1|14, where the breath is controlled through Praanaayaama, where the Mind is kept peaceful and content (Soma also means 'pleasing'), there arises the knowledge of the Lord, i.e., the Lord will provide enlightenment with great light, as told in verse 2|3, at the end of this Maanasika Yaga (mental self-control), just as the well-lit fire of a Yajna spreads intense light all around.

सविता प्रसवेन जुषेत ब्रह्म पूर्व्यम् ।
तत्र योनिं कृणवसे न हि ते पूर्वमक्षिपत् ॥२।७॥

By the encouragement provided by the Lord (as told in 2|3), you (the seeker) should serve Brahma and the teacher who has already seen Brahma (as given in 2|5). There, you should return to the source/ womb (i.e., he should erase the impressions of his earlier lives, called Sanskaaras, and start afresh with his original purity). Then, your earlier (acquired Sanskaaras) will not hamper you.

When we perform a deed – whether physical, verbal or mental – the act creates an impression on our minds, called Sanskaara. This impression can be broadly classified as attractive or repulsive. Suppose we donate food to a beggar. We usually feel good about the happiness we have spread. We feel like donating again later, because we remember the warmth of satisfaction that the first time had created. This memory is the attractive Sanskaara, called Raaga. It urges us to perform the deed we like again and again. Similarly, suppose that we commit a theft. The guilt of the act creates revulsion in us. Memory of this revulsion is imprinted on our minds and stops us again and again from performing the misdeed. This is a repulsive Sanskaara, called Dwesha.

In normal life we want to establish attractive Sanskaaras towards Dhaarmika deeds as propounded by the Vedas, and repulsive Sanskaaras towards Adhaarmika deeds. However, for the one who wants to connect with God, both are a hurdle, as they both push us towards action in this material world. He has to change both to neutral. Where God resides, there is no attraction or repulsion, but only bliss. The Sanskaaras may be viewed as dirt that covers the pure mirror of our soul. We can see our reflection in it only when that dirt has been cleared.[3] For this, the Yogi gives himself up to his Guru and/or God like a piece of clay, which the teacher can shape as he desires. This is what this verse is exhorting us to do.

In the next three verses, the Rshi elaborates on the procedure for meditation as given in the above five Vaidika verses, adding from his own rich experience –

त्रिरुन्नतं स्थाप्य समं शरीरं
हृदीन्द्रियाणि मनसा सन्निवेश्य।
ब्रह्मोडुपेन प्रतरेत विद्वान्
स्रोतांसि सर्वाणि भयावहानि ॥ २।८॥

(Sitting for meditation,) lifting the three parts (head, neck and chest, i.e., not slouching), keeping the back straight, immersing the senses into the Intellect by means of the Mind (as given in 2|1-5), the knowledgeable seeker should tide over all the fearful streams (of the senses as described in 1|5) by means of the boat that is Brahma (God).

Keeping the body erect, though relaxed, ensures that the meditator does not fall off to sleep. Also, the various poses recommended for the sitting posture in Yoga ensure that one can

3 See verse 2|14.

sit in them for an extended period without any discomfort.

The inputs coming from the senses are like fearful streams for the meditator as they forcefully wrest attention from her goal. As the Veda preached, the seer informs us that the right way to go about meditation is to move our focus of attention from the senses to the Mind, and thence to the Intellect – the internal thought engine. Then, one should immerse oneself in Brahma. This immersion will lead to floatation over the stream of Life!

प्राणान् प्रपीड्येह संयुक्तचेष्टः
क्षीणे प्राणे नासिकयोच्छ्वसीत ।
दुष्टाश्वयुक्तमिव वाहमेनं
विद्वान् मनो धारयेताप्रमत्तः ॥२।९॥

In this position, with his breath controlled (through Praanaayaama), and with his bodily movements in check, he should breathe through the nose with a breath that is almost imperceptible. The learned seeker should control the Mind with great care, as if it is a chariot yoked with wild steed.

The fickleness of the Mind is well-known in Vaidika lore and is often likened to a chariot with five horses, one for each sense. The Mind is portrayed as the reins of the Body-chariot, the Intellect being the charioteer who has direct control over the horses. The Soul is the owner of the chariot, sitting in the passenger-seat. It is up to the Soul to give proper instructions to the charioteer, so that he controls the horses smoothly. Otherwise he will let the horses run amuck![4] The time-tested way to control the Mind is by performing Praanaayaama. This makes the breath long and light, so that it is almost imperceptible. This lends stability to the Mind.[5]

4 *Here's the full metaphor from Kathopanishad –*
आत्मानं रथिनं विद्धि शरीरं रथमेव तु । बुद्धिं तु सारथिं विद्धि मनः प्रग्रहमेव च ॥
इन्द्रियाणि हयानाहुर्विषयांस्तेषु गोचरान् । आत्मेन्द्रियमनोयुक्तं भोक्तेत्याहुर्मनीषिणः ॥कठ०१।३।३-४॥
5 *Modern science should probably look into this linkage between breath and the mind.*

The remaining movements of thought then have to be controlled through mental effort and focussing one's attention on the Divine.

समे शुचौ शर्करावह्निवालुका-
विवर्जिते शब्दजलाश्रयादिभिः ।
मनोऽनुकूले न तु चक्षुपीडने
गुहानिवाताश्रयणे प्रयोजयेत् ॥२।१०॥

The seeker should meditate in a place that is level (not on an incline or uneven), devoid of pebbles, fire, sand and noise, like that from a water-body. The place should be pleasant and not an eyesore. It should be in the nature of a cave with no breeze.

If the meditator sits on a pedestal, there is a danger of his falling, while changing position. If he is on low ground, then that will create a claustrophobic feeling. If the ground is uneven, he is in danger of losing balance. Fire could crackle or create temperature differences, say, as it dies out. Pebbles and sand would also tend to produce instability of posture. The slightest of sound or breeze can distract the senses. So, a cave is ideal for this purpose. Also, in prolonged meditation, the eyes would open now and then. A pleasant scene would not disrupt the mindset of the meditator and only further his efforts.[6]

In the next five verses, the seer tells us about the state of the Yogi – the changes in his internal and external being as his meditation starts bearing fruit.

नीहारधूमार्कानिलानलानां
खद्योतविद्युत्स्फटिकशशीनाम् ।
एतानि रूपाणि पुरःसराणि
ब्रह्मण्यभिव्यक्तिकराणि योगे ॥२।११॥

In this yoking (of the Soul with Brahma), the forms that appear

6 *The many caves carved out by Buddhist and Jain monks that dot the Indian landscape even today stand testimony to this Vaidika practice.*

as early indicators of the impending realisation of Brahma (i.e., indications that the meditation is proceeding well and approaching its goal) are - the sensation of a mist, smoke, the sun, a breeze, or fire, and light like that of fireflies, lightning, a crystal or the moon.

पृथ्व्यप्तेजोऽनिलखे समुत्थिते
पञ्चात्मके योगगुणे प्रवृत्ते ।
न तस्य रोगो न जरा न मृत्युः
प्राप्तस्य योगाग्निमयं शरीरम् ॥ २। १२॥

(As the meditation becomes deeper,) the five-fold properties of the impending union with God arise as control of the five elements - Earth, Water, Heat, Air and Space. Attaining this body imbued with the fire of Yoga, the seeker sheds disease, old age and even death.

The one who has seen the Supreme remains eternally youthful, and controls his departure from the body. These are called Yoga-siddhis.

लघुत्वमारोग्यमलोलुपत्वं
वर्णप्रसादं स्वरसौष्ठवं च ।
गन्धः शुभो मूत्रपुरीषमल्पं
योगप्रवृत्तिं प्रथमां वदन्ति ॥ २। १३॥

The body becomes light and healthy, the meditator loses all greed (attraction towards material objects), her complexion becomes pleasing and the voice sweet. A sweet scent emanates from the body. Urine and faeces (all excretions, in fact) are reduced. The (Brahmavaadis) say that this is the first sign of Yoga (union with Brahma).

यथैव विम्बं मृदयोपलिप्तं
तेजोमयं भ्राजते तत् सुधान्तम् ।
तद्वात्मतत्त्वं प्रसमीक्ष्य देही
एकः कृतार्थो भवते वीतशोकः ॥ २।१४ ॥

Just like a mirror covered with mud, shines radiantly when cleaned, so also when the embodied solitary meditator perceives the 'substance' of his Soul, then he becomes successful in his efforts and sheds all sorrow.

'Krtaarth' is a word used for spiritual success, whether in attaining knowledge, or the blessings of the Guru (mentor), or in perceiving the Self. Here, the latter is the goal of the Yogi, and the above signs indicate he has achieved that goal.

यदात्मतत्त्वेन तु ब्रह्मतत्त्वं
दीपोपमेनेह युक्तः प्रपश्येत् ।
अजं ध्रुवं सर्वतत्त्वैर्विशुद्धं
ज्ञात्वा देवं मुच्यते सर्वपाशैः ॥ २।१५ ॥

Just as a lamp reveals that which is in darkness, so also the Individual Soul reveals the Supreme (when it enters Yoga with Brahma in Samaadhi). Knowing the Divine, who is never born, is always unmoving and unchanging, and is devoid of any impurity arising out of contact with Matter, it is released from all bondage (of the body and of birth and death).

In these two verses, the Soul seeing first itself and then using this platform to view God is detailed most explicitly. It leaves no room for misinterpretation and fudging of meaning. Also, the belief that God takes a bodily form as an Avataara is countered here. People who believe in Avataaras, and yet believe in Moksha, should ponder over why freedom from birth and death should be so important for the Soul, if God Himself is doing the same! Ideally, we should always be following in His footsteps. But then, it is so much easier for all of us to follow the well-trodden path that others are following than question where it is leading...

The seer now picks up one more verse from Yajurveda (32|4)[7] to describe this unique entity called God –

एष ह देवः प्रदिशोऽनु सर्वाः
पूर्वो ह जातः स उ गर्भे अन्तः ।
स एव जातः स जनिष्यमाणः
प्रत्यङ् जनास्तिष्ठति सर्वतोमुखः ॥२।१६॥

This Divine Being permeates all the cardinal directions and the sub-directions (i.e., all of space). It is the first to be 'born', i.e., to be revealed, to wake up in this womb (signifying the Universe). He alone is revealed (first), and He is the One who will always be revealed (first) in the future (Universes as well). He resides in every part of every organism with His face in all directions (i.e., there is no place and no being that is not observed by Him at all times).

In effect, the verse explains how the Soul begins to see the Divine. It starts perceiving God as pervading all of Space and Time, and observing everything at all times.

There should not be any confusion regarding the usage of the word 'born' in the context of God. Very obviously, the womb being talked about here is not that of a mother, otherwise God could not be the first one to be born, the mother would have to have come earlier! In a very philosophical sense, 'being born' is being revealed. At birth, the baby reveals itself to the world, having hidden itself in the womb so long. At an even deeper level, the birth of a baby reveals the Soul that it encapsulates, for the Soul by itself cannot be seen. Similarly, God reveals Himself by creating the Universe. Till then there is nobody to see Him. Now, he becomes visible surrounded by the body of the Universe.

7 *The only difference in the Vaidika mantra is that '*एष*' is written as '*एषो*' there.*

The seer ends the second chapter with a eulogy and complete submission to God –

यो देवो अग्नौ यो अप्सु यो विश्वं भुवनमाविवेश ।
य ओषधीषु यो वनस्पतिषु तस्मै देवाय नमो नमः ॥२।१७॥

The Divine One who is present in fire, the One who is present in the waters, the One who permeates all locations where beings exist, the One who is present in all the seasonal plants and the perennial ones, many salutations to that Divine Being!

This is how an enlightened person sees God in all of Creation!

CHAPTER THREE

The Nature of Brahma

❧

In this chapter, Shwetaashwatara describes in great detail the nature and functions of God, or Brahma, or Isha, or Rudra, or any of the other names that describe Him. This knowledge is imperative for the seeker to strive for and to attain Him.

य एको जालवानीशत ईशनीभिः
सर्वाँल्लोकानीशत ईशनीभिः ।
य एवैक उद्भवे सम्भवे च
य एतद्विदुरमृतास्ते भवन्ति ॥३।१॥

He alone is the single entity who has spread the net (of bondage through the Cycle of Birth and Death, ensnaring the Soul in a material jail in the form of a body) and rules over it by the powers at His command (apportioning happiness and sorrow to all beings in their respective jails). He lords over all the heavenly objects by his powers (thus running the Universe in an orderly fashion). He, alone and single, presides over the Universe in its beginning and during its existence (and, by implication, in its dissolution). The wise one, knowing Him as such, attains salvation.

Describing the powers of God as the Creator, Maintainer and Destroyer of the Universe, the verse also lays stress on His oneness and the fact that the seeker needs to know these attributes in order to be relieved of his bondage from the material body.

Further describing the role of God in Creation and stressing His oneness, the seer says -

एको हि रुद्रो न द्वितीयाय तस्थुर्-
य इमाँल्लोकानीशत ईशनीभीः ।
प्रत्यङ् जनांस्तिष्ठति संचुकोचान्तकाले
संसृज्य विश्वा भुवनानि गोपाः ॥ ३ । २ ॥

The One who lords over the heavenly objects through the powers at His command is Rudra and is verily single. (The wise) do not stand for a second (God). The Protector, after creating all the heavenly bodies (at the beginning of the Universe), resides in every part of every living thing. In the end, He shrinks the whole Universe (back to its original state).

Rudra is the name of God that denotes the One who makes people cry, since He is the One who metes out sorrows to Souls based on their deeds.

Gopaa does *not* refer to the protector of cows! 'Go' is a term used also for the senses, for light, for planets - our own one in particular, etc. Here, the meaning is 'the Universe'. 'Gopaa' then becomes the Protector of the Universe. Thus, God not only creates the Universe, but also protects it (Gopaa), shaping it so that it supports life. He then takes up residence inside each being and not only protects that being, but also metes out happiness and sorrow to it based on the being's own actions (as Rudra).

The verse lays great emphasis on the oneness of God. It lays down that the wise can in no way accept a second God that may be required to help Him run the Universe, or as a counter to Him in the form of a devil. Until we are deluded and think that we are in command over our world, or that many gods are in control of different things, and/

or there is a devil who is in conflict with God, or that the order in the Universe is natural and owes nothing to anybody, till that time we cannot expect salvation. The comprehension of the ultimate truth is a necessary condition for the ultimate release from bondage.

The verse also lays down the Vaidika concept of the Cycle of the Universe - its creation (Srshti), its maintenance/expansion (Kalpa) and its dissolution (Pralaya), when all Matter returns to its primordial state and all Souls lie in limbo. God alone stays awake, though inactive. With the start of the next Universe, he rises again. The Big Bang is clearly hinted at here by the words 'He shrinks the Universe' at the time of Pralaya.[1]

The importance of the next verse can be gauged from the fact that it is to be found in the Rg (10|81|3), the Yajur (17|19) *and* the Atharva (13|26) Vedas.

विश्वतश्चक्षुरुत विश्वतोमुखो
विश्वतोबाहुरुत विश्वतस्पात् ।
सं बाहुभ्यां धमति सं पतत्रैर्-
द्यावाभूमी जनयन् देव एकः ॥ ३।३॥

The Divine Being is one and has eyes, mouth, arms and legs everywhere (in this Universe). Creating the luminous and the non-luminous bodies (in the Universe) by the particles that have the capacity to move[2] (i.e., the atoms and other sub-atomic particles, and photons), He pervades Creation with great power and strength (His two 'arms').

Eyes denote the power of sight, or, by extension, knowing. Thus, He sees all and knows all. The mouth denotes the power of speech, i.e., His sermon to all beings about how to transact in this world, is available to everyone, everywhere and at all times. Arms

---

1 *Ref. Introduction, point 2.*
2 *This insightful meaning of 'Patatra', which is usually understood as 'wing', was given by Swami Dayananda Saraswati of the Arya Samaja in his commentary on the Vedas, written in the later 1870s.*

represent physical power, and legs physical reach. Thus, the verse describes God as Omniscient, the Great Preacher, Omnipotent and Omnipresent.

From the proximity of the terms 'power' and 'particles, luminous and non-luminous bodies and radiation', we may also surmise that the latter themselves encompass a lot of power within themselves. In fact, if not understood thus, the concept of power would have to be considered a repetition in the verse, which is frowned upon in the Shaastras, particularly the Vedas. This extension of meaning derived from the proximity of words is a peculiarity of the Vedas.

Elaborating on the above loaded Vaidika verse, Shwetaashwatara says–

यो देवानां प्रभवश्चोद्भवश्च
विश्वाधिपो रुद्रो महर्षिः ।
हिरण्यगर्भः जनयामास पूर्वं
स नो बुद्ध्या शुभया संयुनक्तु ॥ ३ । ४ ॥

He who is the Creator and Expander of all the natural forces and elements in this Universe, He who is the Lord of all, who controls everyone and is the Great Seer, He is the One Who created, in the beginning, the Hiranyagarbha (the intensely luminous early Universe from which this existing Universe has evolved). May He bestow auspicious knowledge on us!

The word 'Deva', used in the singular for God in the last verse and also in many other previous verses, is used in the plural here. It denotes the natural forces, like the gravitational force, electromagnetic force, etc., and the five elements, which together make up this Universe. This is because each of them has unique or 'divine' properties.[3]

The word 'Hiranyagarbha' is found often in the Vedas. It typically

---

3 *The personification of Agni, Vayu, Jala, etc., as Devas or demi-gods living in a heaven not accessible to mere mortals is a mythological concept propounded by the Puranas, which has origins in this Vaidika meaning, but has placed them in a human garb.*

means the Universe, because the Universe holds many intensely luminous bodies (Hiranya) inside it (denoted as Garbha, or womb). It could also mean God, because God holds the Universe itself inside Him. Here, the qualifying word 'Poorvam' reveals that the verse is talking about the early universe. Astronomers today have come to realize that the Universe became intensely bright soon after the Big Bang, called the Photon Epoch.[4]

The seer tells us that the Intellect is also controlled by the Lord to some extent. Therefore, we seek His blessings that our knowledge be righteous (Dhaarmika) and lead us towards Dharma, and away from Adharma. This line is carried as a refrain in some future verses as well.

The following verse from the Yajurveda (16|2)[5] addresses the Lord as Rudra, the One who makes the wicked cry –

या ते रुद्र शिवा तनूरघोरापापकाशिनी ।
तया नस्तनुवा शन्तमया गिरिशन्ताभिचाकशीहि ॥ ३ । ५॥

O Rudra ! O Girishanta! That body of yours, which is auspicious and does not generate fear, but instead illumines the path of righteousness, with that body, please gaze at us.

At the superficial level, this verse is asking God to divert His angry gaze reserved for the wicked, and to look at us with a benevolent gaze. However, it has a deeper meaning, too.

The word 'Shivaa', or benevolent, is an adjective to 'Tanoo' meaning 'body'. Here, the body means the world around us. Thus, 'Shivaa Tanoo' means – May everything in this world be benevolent towards us!

'Girishanta' refers to the One with benevolent speech (Giri is derived from the same root verb from which Giraa, or speech, is

---

4 *https://en.wikipedia.org/wiki/Chronology_of_the_universe*
5 *In the Vaidika mantra,* 'तनुवा' *is given as* 'तन्वा'.

derived). At a deeper level, 'Girishanta' means the One Who spreads auspiciousness through His speech. This He does in two ways – one, through our conscience and two, by means of the Vedas.

The verse then means: O Lord who tells me about Dharma by means of the teachings of the Vedas, please look at me kindly, so that only good things befall me in this world! I know that while you are Rudra, who will make me cry if I do not follow your path, you are also the Benevolent One, who has preached Dharma – the difference between right and wrong – to all mankind in the form of the Vedas and my conscience. Please preach to me that auspicious sermon of yours again and again, so that I follow the path of Dharma and am never at the receiving end of your ire.[6]

The next verse, also the next in Yajurveda (16|3), continues the thought from the previous verse –

यामिषुं गिरिशन्त हस्ते बिभर्ष्यस्तवे ।
शिवां गिरित्र तां कुरु मा हिंसीः पुरुषं जगत् ॥ ३ । ६ ॥

O Girishanta and the Protector of those who preach righteousness (Giritra)! Please make auspicious the arrow (of the Law of Karma) that is held in your hand and is ready to be discharged (at me and the rest of the living world). Please do not hurt the living world (i.e., any living being)!

In the last two verses, the Soul beseeches God to be benevolent and not inflict pain on it. But it does not ask God to forgive its sins, but to preach the path of righteousness to it, so that it may not be *necessary* for it to be punished. This is the essence that is encapsulated in the fourth quarter of 3|4.

The weapon in the hands of God is the Law of Karma by which he distributes happiness or sorrow based on a person's actions in life.

---

6 *The word 'Shivaa' here reveals the origin of the myth of Shiva and his third eye! Also, the usage of the word 'Giri' develops into the Kailash Parvat in the Puranas!*

The verse not only pleads to God to make this 'arrow' an instrument of joy rather than grief, but also asks this for the whole world. This is the elevated thinking of the ancient seers!

This particular verse also implies that God protects those who preach righteousness, and so also must we protect them, as it is from them that we learn right from wrong. Also, inherent is the meaning that those who have discovered the rightful path must preach it to others.

Purusha means that which lies in, or resides in, a Puri - a residence, or a town. Usually, the word denotes God, who resides in the Universe, or, the Soul, that occupies the body. Strangely, the word has been used as an adjective of Jagat, i.e., the Universe. Here, it denotes living beings – those that stay in this Universe. Hence, the meaning 'the living world'.

Returning to the thought of 3|4, the sage says –

ततः परं ब्रह्मपरं बृहन्तं
यथानिकायं सर्वभूतेषु गूढम् ।
विश्वस्यैकं परिवेष्टितारम्-
ईशं तं ज्ञात्वामृता भवन्ति ॥ ३।७॥

The One who is beyond (the above-mentioned world of living beings), is beyond even the Vedas, is gigantic, is hidden inside all living things (as if) according to their size, is the Enveloper of everything, is the Lord of all. Knowing this Lord, the seers attain immortality.

While 'TataH Param' has been described as 'beyond the world' by referring to the words 'Purusham Jagat' from the earlier verse, it also continues from 3|4 as "After having created the Universe, He hid Himself among the beings". This 'hiding among the beings according to their body' tells us that He exists in every part of every living thing and is always watching all its thoughts, speech and actions, giving it its due and encouraging it towards good deeds. Also, He envelopes the beings, thus covering them from inside and outside, leaving no space without Him.

To attain salvation, it is absolutely essential to get some understanding of Him.

The following ardent prayer from the Yajurveda (31|18) is worth including in one's daily prayers. It speaks of the experience of God by a seer on the one hand, but also speaks of a devotee's desire to attain that state –

वेदाहमेतं पुरुषं महान्तम्-
आदित्यवर्णं तमसः परस्तात्।
तमेव विदित्वाति मृत्युमेति
नान्यः पन्था विद्यतेऽयनाय ॥ ३।८॥

I have come to know (or, may I come to know) this Purusha (the One who resides throughout this Universe and even beyond), who is Great, who is the colour of the Sun (i.e., self-luminous like the Sun), who is beyond the darkness (of ignorance), (because) knowing Him alone does one go beyond death. There exists no other path to immortality.

The Supreme is often called light or associated with light in some way. Light is a powerful metaphor for knowledge. Seers are often shown with a halo of light encircling their heads. God, being Omniscient, is the most radiant of all. Also, to the seeker, God *appears* as light. That is why God is always associated with light, even though darkness is also filled with Him.

In spiritual pursuit, many paths are seemingly available today. It is a fashion to be all-inclusive, to say that this path is also right and so is its opposite. But these paths do not converge! This is a falsity in order to gain more disciples and earn more money. Just like truth,[7] the path of righteousness and the path to salvation are only one; there are no alternate paths, no alternate truths, no alternate realities, no alternate gods. For the true seeker, separating the grain from the chaff is the biggest hurdle today. The Vedas specify that

7 Ref. 1|15 for an exposition on why truth is only one.

single path which leads to salvation – knowledge of God through meditation. All others lead to other destinations – good or bad.

Overcome with Bhakti (devotion) for the Supreme, the sage sings forth –

यस्मात् परं नापरमस्ति किंचिद्
   यस्मान्नाणीयो न ज्यायोऽस्ति कश्चित् ।
वृक्ष इव स्तब्धो दिवि तिष्ठत्येकस्-
   तेनेदं पूर्णं पुरुषेण सर्वम् ॥ ३।९॥

There is none greater than that One, nor anyone His equal; there is nothing subtler than Him, nor larger. He stands in light (from His own luminescence), still like a tree. With that Purusha (God), everything (i.e., the Purusha that is the Universe mentioned in 3|6) is completely filled.

Again, the seer urges that God is One and should not be mistaken for many. Also, we see how light is associated with God again.

The analogy with a tree is most beautiful. A tree never moves, yet brings forth flowers and fruits for the good of others, keeping nothing for itself. Because God is Omnipresent, there is no movement possible in Him. He desires nothing. Yet, He creates this whole Universe and maintains it for the good of all.

ततो यदुत्तरतरं तदरूपमनामयम् ।
य एतद्विदुरमृतास्ते भवन्त्यथेतरे दुःखमेवापियन्ति ॥ ३।१०॥

That Supreme, which is far beyond the aforesaid Universe, is without form and without defects. Those who knows It as such become immortal, while the others are afflicted with sorrow (in the Cycle of Life and Death).

There are those who believe that giving a form to God helps in visualizing Him. The fact is that when you use a form to visualize Him, you are visualizing the form and not Him! If you feel parental love looking at images of Krishna eating butter, it is because you are visualizing a human child (your child?) and not God. It is inappropriate to replace one thing with another in the quest for truth. In algebra, we replace an unknown value with an 'x' and proceed to find the real value taking this placeholder along. Similarly, in our search for God, we operate with the placeholder 'God' and operate with the properties that the seers have told us exist in it. We then follow the processes they have told us, till we are able to see Him and get rid of the placeholder. Assigning imaginary figures, images, locations, etc., to Him is like assigning a value to x – it does not lead directly to the correct answer!

Explaining the Vaidika verse at 3|3 in his own words, the seer says –

सर्वाननशिरोग्रीवः सर्वभूतगुहाशयः ।
सर्वव्यापी स भगवांस्तस्मात् सर्वगतः शिवः ॥ ३। ११॥

The Supreme has his mouth (advice), head (vision) and neck (movement) in all directions. He lies hidden in the cave (of the Soul) of all living beings. He is Omnipresent and the Owner of all the wealth in the Universe. Therefore, He is called the Auspicious One who has been everywhere and who has got everything (Sarvagata).

An omnipresent mouth implies that God's teachings are available at every location in the Universe. It is not as if you go in space and your conscience will not stop you from committing a crime! He will keep whispering in your mind to show you the right path. An omnipresent head implies that God is watching us everywhere, not only from outside, but also from within. An omnipresent neck implies movement. He is not restricted to any space, and can turn whichever way He wants. These descriptions are only symbolic as God does not really have a head and neck, for if He had a neck in reality, would it be possible to have an eye there?! These are just to help us get our head around some of His many unusual qualities.

We often say that this belongs to us or that belongs to us. We forget that, in reality, nothing belongs to us at all! In the ultimate analysis, God has just 'leased' it out to us for the duration of our lifetime. When the time comes, it will all return to Him.

While sometimes He seems like Rudra to us, He is actually always Shiva, for He always does what is the best for us, who are His children.

The seer motivates the seeker towards attaining Him -

महान् प्रभुर्वै पुरुषः सत्त्वस्यैष प्रवर्तकः ।
सुनिर्मलामिमां प्राप्तिमीशानो ज्योतिरव्ययः ॥ ३। १२॥

That Purusha[8] is Great and the Lord of all. He motivates the intellect (Sattva = Buddhi) (towards attaining Him), an attainment that is wonderfully purifying. He rules over everything, is self-luminous and does not deplete or decay.

As we saw earlier (verse 3|4), since God controls all of Matter, He does have some control on the mind/intellect, too. For this reason, prayer after prayer seeks motivation from God in the right direction – the path of Dharma and the path of salvation.

The seeker has to continuously purify herself in the journey towards God, and when the goal is reached, the last remnants of impurity are automatically shed off.

Since our own body grows and decays, we sometimes imagine God also passing through the phases of infancy, adulthood and old age. However, this is only our imagination. God stays constant and unchanging at all times.

Further detailing the path of attainment, the sage informs -

8 *Refer to 3|6 for meaning.*

अङ्गुष्ठमात्रः पुरुषोऽन्तरात्मा
सदा जनानां हृदये सन्निविष्टः ।
हृदा मन्वीशो मनसाभिक्लृप्तो
य एतद्विदुरमृतास्ते भवन्ति ॥ ३ । १३ ॥

This Purusha is the size of the thumb and resides inside everything, particularly the Soul. He is always to be found hidden inside the heart/ mind of living things. The Lord of the Mind is to be attained by the heart and the mind. Those who come to know Him, become immortal.

Obviously, That which is larger than the Universe and is Omnipresent within it cannot be the size of the thumb! Also, the word 'heart' often means the mind or the intellect. Actually, this metaphor refers to a region within the human brain which is the size of the thumb, meditating upon which leads to enlightenment. The significance of this region is that this is where the Soul resides. Focussing on this region, we first find our self and then, with further practice, see the Lord within us.

The following two verses are found in the Rgveda (10|90|1-2), as also the Purusha Sukta (31|1-2) of the Yajurveda and Atharvaveda (19|6|1-2).[9] In them, the Supreme is referred to as the Purusha. Of course, the seer has also used the same metaphor in the previous few verses as well.

सहस्रशीर्षा पुरुषः सहस्राक्षः सहस्रपात् ।
स भूमिं विश्वतो वृत्वात्यतिष्ठद्दशाङ्गुलम् ॥ ३ । १४ ॥

That Purusha has a thousand (i.e., infinite) heads, eyes and feet inside Him (i.e., those of the living beings that He is enveloping).[10] Having

---

9 *The verses of Yajurveda and Atharvaveda read with a difference of word or two, with no substantial change in the meaning of the verse.*

10 *While the usual interpretation of the words 'Sahasrasheersha, Sahasraaksha, Sahasrapaat' refers to the 'One who has a thousand heads, eyes and feet', and this is the meaning that Shwetaashwatara himself seems to have accepted (in verse 3|16), Swami Dayanand Saraswati has given a variation in the meaning which seems more suited to the rest of the verse. That is, thus, the meaning given here.*

enveloped the Earth from all sides, He stays beyond the Ten Fingers (i.e., the ten forms of Matter, viz, the five gross elements [Sthoolbhootas] and the five subtle forms of these elements [Sookshmabhootas]).

The Earth may be taken as the planet where we reside. But, in a more generic sense, Bhoomi represents all the locations (Lokas) where beings reside in the Universe.

'Stays beyond Matter' implies that, even though God envelopes Matter, and even pervades it, He remains distinct from it. Never do the two become one.

पुरुष एवेदं सर्वं यद्भूतं यच्च भव्यम् ।
उतामृत्वस्येशानो यदेन्नेनातिरोहति ॥ ३ । १५॥

This Purusha is all that is there – whether it be that which is past, or that which is the future (and, by implication, that which is the present). He is the Lord of the immortal and of that which grows by food.

The identity of the Purusha with Time is to signify His complete control of this parameter and all that is bound by it. While the previous verse defined His all-pervasiveness, this verse shows Him to be the Supreme Controller of Time and all things affected by it.

The second line has two meanings. Firstly, God lords over the Souls who have attained immortality (Amrta) through salvation vis a vis those who have not and are trapped in this world as living beings growing by means of food. Secondly, God also controls the everlasting primordial Matter (also Amrta), which transforms into the objects of the Universe, ending in various forms of food (Anna). This, thus, covers all the three parts of the Universe – the Souls that have achieved salvation, those that inhabit this world and Matter. Again, we are witness to the beauty and expanse of the meaning of a Vaidika verse!

Shwetaashwatara now explains verse 3|14 himself –

सर्वतः पाणिपादं तत् सर्वतोऽक्षिशिरोमुखम् ।
सर्वतः श्रुतिमल्लोके सर्वमावृत्य तिष्ठति ॥ ३ । १६॥

*The Supreme has hands and feet in all directions, as also eyes, head,
mouth and ears (refer to 3/3 and 3/11 for the meaning of each organ
in the context of God). In the Universe It exists, enveloping everything.*

Seemingly contradicting the earlier verse, the sage clarifies –

सर्वेन्द्रियगुणाभासं सर्वेन्द्रियविवर्जितम् ।
सर्वस्य प्रभुमीशानं सर्वस्य शरणं बृहत् ॥ ३ । १७॥

*(Even though) It has no sense organs per se, It has the capability
to perceive the property of each of the senses. It is the Lord and Ruler
of all, and also the Great Refuge of all.*

From this, it should be clear that when God was said to have a
mouth or an ear everywhere, it was only a metaphorical description.
He has this amazing property of being able to perceive everything
in every 'point' of His being.

The Supreme is the greatest refuge for Souls. He is with us at
all times – when nobody else is there, He is by our side. He is also
capable of changing things that are overwhelming us. If this were
not so, it would be quite meaningless to pray to Him for change.
Because He is so kind, He does make subtle changes when we pray
fervently to Him, and makes our fate more bearable for us.

The sage now draws upon the Vaidika metaphor of the human
body as a city –

नवद्वारे पुरे देही हंसो लेलायते बहिः ।
वशी सर्वस्य लोकस्य स्थावरस्य चरस्य च ॥ ३ । १८॥

The Hansa (God) stays within this body that is (like) a city of nine doors, and also is resplendent outside it. He is the Controller of all living beings, whether they be immobile (plants) or mobile (all other creatures).

The human body has 9 openings – 2 for the eyes, 2 for the ears, 2 nostrils, 1 mouth, 1 urethra and 1 anus. Therefore, the human body is called 'the city of nine doors'.

While in verse 1|6, the Soul had been called Hansa, in this verse God has been called the same. We saw in that verse that the word originates from the root 'Han' which means 'to destroy/harm' and 'to move'. Both meanings are applicable here – God is called Hansa because He moves everything in the Universe and also because He punishes the wicked by causing them harm.

It may be noted here that, in India, from time immemorial, plants are known to be life-forms.

Further elaborating the thought of 3|17, the sage composes this lovely verse –

अपाणिपादो जवनो ग्रहीता
पश्यत्यचक्षुः स शृणोत्यकर्णः ।
स वेत्ति वेद्यं न च तस्यास्ति वेत्ता
तमाहुरग्र्यं पुरुषं महान्तम् ॥ ३ । १९ ॥

He has no hands or feet. Yet, He is a fast Mover and a Grasper (of all). He sees without eyes and hears without ears. He knows everything worthy of being known, but there is none who comprehends Him. (The learned) call Him the Foremost, the Purusha[11] and the Great.

This beautiful verse describing the enigma that is God is surely worth memorizing!

Continuing in the same vein, the seer also gives the result of seeing the Supreme –

11 Refer 3|6 for meaning.

अणोरणीयान् महतो महीया-
नात्मा गुहायां निहितोऽस्य जन्तोः ।
तमक्रतुं पश्यति वीतशोको
धातुः प्रसादान् महिमानमीशम् ॥ ३।२० ॥

The Soul (Paramaatmaa, i.e., God) is smaller than the smallest, and larger than the largest. He is hidden in the 'cave' (of the intellect) of this living being. (When the wise man,) through God's own grace, sees Him who performs no deed, who is Great and who is the Lord of all, (then) he becomes devoid of all sorrow.

Indian philosophical texts tell us that Matter is the grossest particle, the Soul is subtler and God is the subtlest. That thought is corroborated here. Also, the verse tells us that God exists beyond the Universe, too. That is why an expanding Universe does not require God to change His dimensions!

The metaphor of 'the cave of the intellect or the Soul' is a very common one, even found in the Vedas. This is so due to multiple reasons. Firstly, Yogis typically sought the refuge of caves for their meditation, as we saw in verse 2|10, in order to obtain the necessary quietude. More importantly, when one starts going into meditation, it is as if one enters a cave where the signals from the senses can no longer disturb the Soul. It is in this state that one can achieve God.

While the Universe itself is created and is managed by God – both creation and management involving actions, He is still called the One who performs no deed (Akratu) because He performs all these actions for others, not for Himself. Thus, all His actions are always Nishkaama,[12] without any motive for Himself. He is complete in Himself and does not need any external benefits.

While the Soul usually performs actions towards an end, the success or failure of the enterprise lies with God, as the Gita has famously proclaimed: 'कर्मण्येवाधिकारस्ते' This is also true for seeing

---

12 Refer to 6|4 for more details about Nishkaama Karmas.

God. A Sanyaasi can perform meditation and live an austere life towards that goal, but finally, it is God who will decide when the time has come to give the Bhakta his reward. And the moment he reveals Himself to the devotee, that Soul will shed all desires, thus going beyond sorrow.

Again, a verse worth memorizing!

This next verse is the counterpart of 3|8, but is not a Vaidika verse –

वेदाह्मेतमजरं पुराणं
सर्वात्मानं सर्वगतं विभुत्वात्।
जन्मनिरोधं प्रवदन्ति यस्य
ब्रह्मवादिनो हि प्रवदन्ति नित्यम्॥३।२१॥

I know the One who never becomes old, is very ancient, is the Soul of everything, has reached everywhere because He is Omnipresent. Those who ponder over Brahma say that He never takes birth (the way the Individual Soul does, i.e., by association with Matter) and is eternal.

Being the 'soul of everything' implies that, being subtler than everything else, He occupies the interstices between everything.

The verse refutes explicitly the doctrine of incarnation of God, or Avataara. Sometimes confusion is created when it is said that the seeker, upon seeing God, becomes one with Him. In these instances, one should only read it as an Alankaara, a metaphor, just as two lovers are said to have become one. To think that only part of God is omnipresent, or omniscient, and the rest is limited by a material body as an ignorant Soul, is to delude oneself! A belief in a God with form also lends itself to a belief in many Gods, an abhorrent concept for the Vaidika philosophers.

CHAPTER FOUR

The Trinity

❧

In this chapter, Shwetaashwatara, while continuing to describe God, dwells also on the Individual Soul and Matter, and the relationship between the three.

य एकोऽवर्णो बहुधा शक्तियोगात्
वर्णाननेकान् निहितार्थो दधाति ।
वि चैति चान्ते विश्वमादौ स देवः
स नो बुद्ध्या शुभया संयुनक्तु ॥४।१॥

The One who is but one and without any colour, by His many types of strength, dons many colours (i.e., He creates this multifarious Universe) in the beginning (of Time) for a hidden reason. In the end, that Divine Being also resolves it (back into primordial Matter). May He (who has such immense powers), conjoin us with an intellect that is auspicious!

Again we find a contradiction in terms – the One without colour dons many colours! This is a common practice in spiritual texts, where seers could easily handle such seeming contradictions.

Colour refers to variation in type. While God is Ekarasa – uniform at all points of His being, Matter that is uniform at the beginning of Creation is split up into many types, each type having different 'powers', like electrical charge, mass, gravity, etc. These help the Universe to evolve into the complex structure we see today. All the different objects are then as garments to God, and one can visualize them as the 'colours of God'. At the time of Pralaya (dissolution), this same Universe is again torn to shreds and returned to its uniform state.

The 'hidden reason' implies that His motive in constructing this Universe is hidden from direct investigation. We are unable to comprehend the reason by studying the Universe by itself. Only the Vedas and related scriptures guide us towards it.

The following is a Vaidika verse from the Yajurveda (32|1)[1] –

तदेवाग्निस्तदादित्यस्तद्वायुस्तदु चन्द्रमाः ।
तदेव शुक्रं तद्ब्रह्म तदापस्तत् प्रजापतिः ॥४।२॥

It (the Supreme) alone is Agni (Fire, in its most basic meaning), It is Aaditya (sun), Vaayu (wind), Chandramaa (moon), Shukra (various stars and heavenly bodies), Brahma (the Gigantic One or the Universe), Aapa (the waters) and Prajaapati (Lord of all living beings).

Continuing the metaphor of God donning different 'colours', the seer quotes the Vaidika verse to show that all the objects in the Universe represent It, while It also lords over all of them, including the living beings.

In the original Vaidika context, the words have even deeper meanings. Agni is the One who was revealed first in the Universe, is Self-luminous or Omniscient, and the Giver of knowledge to all. Aaditya is the One who engulfs everything at the end of the Universe. Vaayu is the One with immense strength. Chandramaa is the eternally blissful One and the Giver of bliss. Shukra is the One who operates quickly or the One who is pure. Brahma is the

---

1 In the original Vaidika verse, 'तदापस्तत् प्रजापतिः' reads as 'ता आपः स प्रजापतिः', with no change in meaning.

Immense One. The verse, then, also implies that all these epithets refer to God in Vaidika verses, calling It by different names to focus on the qualities denoted by the name, as given above. There is a belief today that the Vedas propound natural forces as Gods and encourage practices such as fire-worship. This verse roundly counters this view.

Another verse from the Vedas, the Atharva Veda (10|8|27) this time, says –

त्वं स्त्री त्वं पुमानसि त्वं कुमार उत वा कुमारी ।
त्वं जीर्णो दण्डेन वञ्चसि त्वं जातो भवसि विश्वतोमुखः ॥ ४ । ३ ॥

You are a woman and you are a man; you are the youth and the young girl; when old, you move around with a stick; when you are born you have your face everywhere (Omniscient in Creation).

In the current context of God, this is interpreted as He resides in all phases and all genders of life, knowing all the thoughts and actions of each and every being.

In the Veda, the verse is actually for the Individual Soul, stating clearly that the Soul has no gender itself, but acquires that of the body; it has no age and yet acquires that of the body; and birth in different species gives it many different faces.

Elaborating on the metaphor of colours mentioned in verse 4|1, the sage says –

नीलः पतङ्गो हरितो लोहिताक्षस्-
तडिद्गर्भ ऋतवः समुद्राः ।
अनादिमत्त्वं विभुत्वेन वर्तसे
यतो जातानि भुवनानि विश्वा ॥ ४ । ४ ॥

O Lord! You are the blue bee, the green (parrot) with red eyes, the cloud with lightning in its womb, the seasons and the seas. You are without a beginning and exist pervasively in all the heavenly bodies that arise from you.

The implication of God 'acquiring colours' becomes very clear here. He himself does not transform into these objects, but gives 'colour', as it were, to primordial Matter while creating this Universe. However, He exists in all of these through His omnipresence. Therefore, at a gross level, these may be seen as proof of His existence.

The sage expands on the colour metaphor, and paints the other entities in the Universe with his brush –

अजामेकां लोहितशुक्लकृष्णां

बह्वीः प्रजाः सृजमानां सरूपाः ।

अजो ह्येको जुषमाणोऽनुशेते

जहात्येनां भुक्तभोगामजोऽन्यः ॥४।५॥

There is one she-goat that is red, white and black. It creates many children in its own likeness. There is one he-goat that enjoys (the association with the she-goat) and lies with it. Another he-goat, having enjoyed the pleasures of her company, gives her up.

'Prakrti' (Nature) is a feminine word. Therefore, primordial Matter is usually referred to in the feminine. The words 'Aja' and 'Ajaa', while simply meaning the he- and she-goat, respectively, also mean the unborn one.[2] The implication is that Matter is unborn. She has the qualities of red Raja, white Sattva and black Tama[3]. These same qualities are transmitted to all the objects in the Universe, including the bodies of living beings – the children of Matter. The other unborn one – Aja – is the Individual Soul, often referred to in the masculine, as the word 'Atman' is so in Sanskrit. The verse describes two types of Souls. One set of Souls indulges in the pleasures of this world, while a much smaller set has had their fill

---

2 *Compare with verse 1|9.*

3 *Please refer to verse 5|7 for details of Sattva, Raja and Tama.*

of worldly pleasures and forsake them for a higher goal – Brahma!

The fact that Matter and the Soul are 'unborn' highlights the fact that they are not metamorphosed out of God, but exist independently to begin with. This is another myth extremely prevalent among spiritualists today.

This verse is often quoted by scholars to describe the three entities of the Universe.

The following is a Vaidika verse (Rg 1|164|20, Atharva 9|9|20, Mundaka 3|1|1) that describes the relationship between the three eternal entities by means of a beautiful word picture –

द्वा सुपर्णा सयुजा सखाया
समानं वृक्षं परिषस्वजाते ।
तयोरन्यः पिप्पलं स्वाद्वत्त्य-
नश्नन्नन्यो अभिचाकशीति ॥ ४ । ६ ॥

Two birds, who have beautiful plumage, are related to each other and are good friends, are sitting (actually, 'clinging' in Sanskrit) on the same tree. One of these eats the berries of the tree with great relish, while the other one sits watching it.

The tree here represents Nature, Matter, the world. Its fruits represent the worldly enjoyments available to us. The two birds are God and the Soul. Both are bestowed with remarkable abilities, represented by the metaphor of their beautiful plumage, chief among them being consciousness. Both are eternally linked to each other, and they can never be separated. They are also linked with the world. The Soul indulges in its pleasures – the berries, while God is always observing the Soul's each and every action, never partaking of the 'berries'.

The antiquity of the Vedas and the fact that the Indus Valley civilization was a Vaidika one is proven by an Indus Valley seal that depicts the verse (Pic 1).

Pic 1: A seal from Mohanjodaro depicting verse 4/6

The sage extends the metaphor –

समाने वृक्षे पुरुषो निमग्नो-
ऽनीशया शोचति मुह्यमानः ।
जुष्टं यदा पश्यत्यन्यमीश-
मस्य महिमानमिति वीतशोकः ॥४।७॥

On that common tree, the Purusha (Soul) is immersed (in sensual pleasures). Unable to control (the availability of these pleasures), he grieves. However, when he serves the Lord (worships Him, meditates on Him, not bathe a statue that supposedly represents Him, etc.), he sees this Other, and on seeing Its greatness, he becomes devoid of grief.

Seeing the Other implies seeing oneself, too, as separate from Matter. Once the reality of the three eternal entities is 'seen' by the seer, the Mayaa (delusion) of equating oneself with the body vanishes, all worldly desires fall off and thus, all sorrow is shed. The ultimate goal of the Soul is achieved.

The above two popular verses lay down the three eternal entities and their relationship so succinctly that they should definitely be memorized!

The following is again an oft-quoted Vaidika verse (Rgveda 1|164|39, Atharvaveda 9|10|18), describing the importance of seeing God as elaborated in the previous verse –

ऋचो अक्षरे परमे व्योमन्
यस्मिन् देवा अधि विश्वे निषेदुः ।
यस्तं न वेद किमृचा करिष्यति
य इत् तद्विदुस्त इमे समासते ॥४|८॥

From the Vedas, we know about that God, who is as Pervasive as the sky, who is Indestructible and in whom all the natural objects, like the stars and the planets, the Universe itself, reside. (While the Vedas may preach about this God,) if the seeker does not come to know Him (in person, as it were), what will he do with those Vaidika mantras?! On the other hand, those who come to know Him, they come to reside in Him.

Thus, the verse proclaims that, while the Vedas teach about everything in the Universe, including all aspects of our lives, their most important teaching is that of God. If after studying them, we don't look for Him, and find Him in meditation, there is really little that we have learnt from the Vedas! Finding God is so much more important than worldly prosperity that, actually, there is no comparison between the two.

Another important point alluded to here, and hinted at in some of the previous verses, too, is that God cannot be established decisively by any logical means. He is only proven by the Vedas, or experienced in our heart, or seen by a logic beyond equations. This is why the 'mathematical' scientists always arrive at the conclusion that it is impossible to see the Hand of God in Creation, while the 'biological' scientists can see it in everything they study!

Another verse worth remembering!

The seer adds to the Vaidika verse –

छन्दांसि यज्ञाः क्रतवो व्रतानि
भूतं भव्यं यच्च वेदा वदन्ति।
अस्मान्मायी सृजते विश्वमेतत्
तस्मिंश्चान्यो मायया सन्निरुद्धः ॥४।९॥

The Vedas talk about themselves,[4] the daily Yajna, the special Agnihotras (Kratu) performed bi-annually, annually, etc., the various duties (of the various Aashramas, i.e., phases of life), and about Time – the past, present and future, as also whatever else is worth knowing. These are the things by which the Maayee – the Deluder or the Controller of Maayaa, i.e., God – creates all (in this Universe). And in that (Universe), the other (the Soul) is bound by Maayaa.

The Vedas are unique in that they talk of their own creation. From them, we come to know of their divine origin.

The Vedas consider an average life-span of a hundred years, which is split into four equal parts, representing different phases of life, called Aashramas (exertions). The first one is Brahmacharya-ashrama, which involves the acquisition of knowledge or vocational training, while maintaining a strict discipline in attitude and behaviour, including celibacy. The second phase is called Grhastha-ashrama in which the student gets married after graduation and takes up a householder's responsibilities of family and society. The third phase involves retiring into seclusion for the study and practice of spiritual texts. This is called Vaanaprastha. In the last phase, called Sanyaasa-ashrama, the person gives up even the meagre belongings that stay with him in the earlier phase, works towards enlightenment and goes from place to place preaching sermons to householders, who get little time to accommodate deep

---

4 *Chhanda refers to the poetic metres that the Vaidika verses are written in, but by extension, it also refers to the Vedas themselves.*

study of the scriptures in their daily lives.

It is worth noting that the Vedas are referred to as the repository of all knowledge about this world, including even Time!

The words Mayaa and Mayee used in the verse are explained in the next verse –

मायां तु प्रकृतिं विद्यान्मायिनं तु महेश्वरम् ।
तस्यावयवभूतैस्तु व्याप्तं सर्वमिदं जगत् ॥४।१०॥

Know Matter to be Maayaa, and the Supreme Lord to be the Maayee. (It is as if) He has distributed himself in parts that permeate each of the objects in this Universe.

Thus, Mayaa, or Matter, is itself not an illusion. However, it creates a delusion in the Soul that the Soul is Matter. That is why Matter is called Mayaa. God is the one who is instrumental in creating that delusion. That is why He is called Mayee.

It is as if God has split Himself into each item in a way that is custom-made for it and caters to the item directly. This is just to provide a visualization of God's omniscience. He does not really split Himself!

यो योनिं योनिमधितिष्ठत्येको
        यस्मिन्निदं सं च विचैति सर्वम् ।[5]
तमीशानं वरदं देवमीड्यं
        निचाय्येमां शान्तिमत्यन्तमेति ॥४।११॥

He is the One who supervises each cause present in Creation. He is the One in Whom all (Matter) comes together (forming different shapes and forms), and also the One in Whom it separates (at the time

5 *This line is borrowed from Yajurveda 32|8.*

of dissolution). He who comes to realise Him as the One who is the Lord, the Granter of boons, and the Divine Being worthy of worship, attains everlasting peace.

'Yoni' refers to a cause. From that is derived the meaning of 'the womb' – the cause of birth, and from that 'the species' – sharing a similar womb. Here, the first meaning is the most appropriate, though the third is also applicable – He who lords over each and every being.

It is important to note that every effect in the world is supervised closely by God. Some causes are far-reaching in space and time. God, being the Master of both these entities, sets a series of events into motion that lead to, say, a tsunami millennia later.

Everlasting peace is attained by the seeker who finds God because all agitation is caused by the delusion caused by Mayaa.

The following verse varies just a little from verse 3|4. It emphasises the role of God as a Creator of the Universe –

यो देवानां प्रभवश्चोद्भवश्च

विश्वाधिपो रुद्रो महर्षिः ।

हिरण्यगर्भं पश्यत जायमानं

स नो बुद्ध्या शुभया संयुनक्तु ॥४।१२॥

He who is the Creator and Expander of all the natural forces and elements (Devas) in this Universe, He who is the Lord of all, He who makes the wicked cry and is the Great Seer, (having created the Hiranyagarbha) watches over the evolving Universe. May He bestow auspicious knowledge on us!

यो देवानामधिपो

यस्मिँल्लोका अधिश्रिताः ।

य ईशे अस्य द्विपदश्चतुष्पदः

कस्मै देवाय हविषा विधेम[6] ॥४।१३॥

---

6 *The last two lines are found in many Vaidika mantras, e.g., Yajurveda 23|3.*

He is the Lord of the various forces of Nature, in whom all the habitable places of the Universe are supported. He presides over the bipeds and the quadrupeds (and, by extension, all of Life). We offer our worship through meditation to that Divine One who is Bliss personified, and is the Giver of Bliss.

'Kasmai' usually means 'to whom', but here it translates 'to the Blissful One', as 'Ka' also means 'Aanand'. Thus, the last line does not mean "To which Deva should we give our offerings?", but rather "We give our offerings in the form of Upaasana to the Blissful Lord."[7]

सूक्ष्मातिसूक्ष्मं कलिलस्य मध्ये
विश्वस्य स्रष्टारमनेकरूपम् ।
विश्वस्यैकं परिवेष्टितारं
ज्ञात्वा शिवं शान्तिमत्यन्तमेति ॥ ४ । १४ ॥

In the midst of the (seeming) chaos of the Universe, He is subtler than the subtlest. He is the Creator of all, and (so, seemingly) acquires many forms. He is the One Enveloper of all. Knowing this Auspicious One, (the seeker) attains ultimate peace.

The verse describes the conundrum that is God – what may seem as a disorderly Universe to a casual observer, is actually minutely managed by Him. He has no form and, yet, He seems to acquire all the shapes of the Universe. He is the subtlest in all of Creation, and yet He envelopes everything, too.

Ultimate peace is not attained by 'giving up all desires', because at least one ultimate desire to see one's true self and God will remain. Rather, it is attained only when one gets a vision of God. The fulfilment produced by that vision clears even that last desire and leaves behind pure bliss and peace.

---

7 *The lack of understanding of this second meaning of 'Ka', a word that is frequently used in the Vedas, has led to a lot of misinterpretation of the verses by Western scholars.*

स एव काले भुवनस्य गोप्ता
विश्वाधिपः सर्वभूतेषु गूढः ।
यस्मिन् युक्ता ब्रह्मर्षयो देवताश्च
तमेवं ज्ञात्वा मृत्युपाशांश्छिनत्ति ॥४।१५॥

At all times, He protects the habitation (of living beings), oversees everything, and lies hidden in everything. The knowers of the Vedas and the extremely brilliant ones connect (with Him) inside Him, and, coming to know Him thus, break asunder the snares of Death.

Here, the reference to 'time' denotes the fact that Time, like Space, is a material entity. When there is no Time, He does not need to protect anything, because there is no Creation itself!

He brings about life and then ensures its continuity. As scientists are discovering today, life occurs in an extremely narrow range of parameters, called the Goldilock's Zone. Earth happens to lie in such a zone. This range is first created and then scrupulously maintained.

The seers realise that He resides in the Soul, and that is where they have to find Him. While simple people may feel gratified by visiting holy places, the seeker has to find the true Brahma, and for that, he has to look within.

This next verse repeats many of the concepts already covered, but further elucidates the nature of God through an everyday example –

घृतात् परं मण्डमिवातिसूक्ष्मं
ज्ञात्वा शिवं सर्वभूतेषु गूढम् ।
विश्वस्यैकं परिवेष्टितारं
ज्ञात्वा देवं मुच्यते सर्वपाशैः ॥४।१६॥

He is ultra-fine, like the fine film that floats on top of the butter (when milk is churned.) Knowing this Benevolent One, who is hidden inside all created objects, who is the One Enveloper of all and the Divine, (the seeker) is freed of all bondage.

The world may seem like milk to us, but for the seer it actually consists of butter and water, where he separates the Subtle from the rest by stilling the mind.

The one bondage of a material body creates all other worldly bondages, like the need to eat, drink, sleep, etc. Once the seer acquires Moksha, the Soul itself needs no such material crutches, and the ensuing ephemeral happiness and sorrow. Instead, it finds eternal peace.

The following verse is very similar to 3|13 –

एष देवो विश्वकर्मा महात्मा
सदा जनानां हृदये सन्निविष्टः ।
हृदा मनीषा मनसाभिक्लृप्तो
य एतद्विदुरमृतास्ते भवन्ति ॥४।१७॥

This Divine Great Soul, the Doer of all Deeds (i.e., the creation, maintenance and destruction of this Universe) is always to be found hidden inside the heart/mind of living things. He is to be attained by the heart (= intellect), knowledge (Maneeshaa) and the mind. Those who come to know Him become immortal.

As elaborated earlier (verse 3|13), the heart actually means the intellect. The fact that the Supreme occupies the heart of living beings is emphasized so often, when it is in apparent contradiction to the fact that He actually pervades the smallest to the largest in the Universe. This is to bring out the fact that the seeker should contemplate in the depths of the intellect. In meditation, the seeker has to journey inwards from the senses to the mind to the intellect. The intellect is the one that is directly hooked to the Soul. Once we see our pure selves, we have to peep further inwards to find the Lord. That is the significance of this oft-repeated, seemingly contradictory statement.

Knowledge has been introduced here as another crucial component in the discovery of Brahma. There are some who believe that Bhakti, or devotion to the Divine, is sufficient to attain His grace. But all the Vedas and the Upanishads point to the contrary. Till you have made yourself worthy of His grace, you will not attain Him. He would not give all the knowledge of the Universe in the Vedas, if all we needed to attain our ultimate goal was to start loving a human form, supposedly in his likeness! And we cannot start loving a formless entity till we know Its qualities and Its love for us. This is why all true knowledge is required to understand Him. This is where Vaidika Dharma differs from all religions – there is no dichotomy between science and religion here!

Describing beautifully the state of enlightenment, the seer says –

यदातमस्तन्न दिवा न रात्रिर्-
न सन्न चासच्छिव एव केवलः ।
तदक्षरं तत्सवितुर्वरेण्यं
प्रज्ञा च तस्मात् प्रसृता पुराणी ॥४।१८॥

When the seeker becomes devoid of the darkness (of ignorance, i.e., when he perceives God), there is no day and no night; there is no something (Sat) and no nothing (Asat); there is only Shiva, the Auspicious One, and the One who is single and alone (Kevala)[8]. He is indestructible (Akshara), the Creator worthy of emulation. There is also (within the seeker) the knowledge/intelligence that has emanated from Him since time immemorial.

This Prajnaa, or intelligence, is the one by which we perceive Him, as the normal intelligence is not good enough to see Him. It is given by Him to the ardent seeker ever since mankind has looked for Him. Thus, first the seeker has to study the scriptures, the Vedas, to

---

8 *Refer to 1|11 for a detailed explanation.*

understand and contemplate on the nature of reality and the Self. Once he starts distancing himself from the Matter that envelopes his self, God lends a helping hand and starts unveiling more about Himself and everything else. This is denoted by the word 'Prajnaa'.

The next verse is a combination of two verses from the Yajurveda (line 1 from 32|2 + line 2 from 32|3), and further describes the Shiva mentioned above –

नैनमूर्ध्वं न तिर्यञ्चं न मध्ये परिजग्रभत् ।
न तस्य प्रतिमा अस्ति यस्य नाम महद्यशः ॥४।१९॥

God cannot be grasped from the top (or the bottom), or from the sides, or in the middle (because He has no such regions, and He is too subtle to be held by either the body or the senses). In fact, the One whose name is 'The One of Great Fame' cannot be circumscribed by any image or any other material representation.

No part of the Lord can be grasped, either physically or mentally. We can only get a hazy glimpse of Him, as it were.

Here, 'The One of Great Fame' refers to God's fame being there throughout the Universe. In effect, the Universe itself is His eulogy. Also, the name implies that He is the Giver of great fame to His devotee.

We notice here how the Vedas exhort the seeker that no image should be created of Him for worship, because that only creates a further delusion and departure from the truth.

Elaborating the last line of the previous verse, the seer says –

न संदृशे तिष्ठति रूपमस्य
न चक्षुषा पश्यति कश्चनैनम् ।
हृदा हृदिस्थं मनसा य एनम्-
एवं विदुरमृतास्ते भवन्ति ॥४।२०॥

His form cannot be encompassed by any vision; nobody can perceive Him through his eyes. He resides in the heart/intellect. Those who perceive Him through the heart/intellect and the mind in this way become immortal.

Those who 'see' Him actually feel His presence within their selves, and are well aware that they have not seen or understood even a fraction of Him, just as one looks at the ocean and has no doubts that she is not seeing the whole, but only a part of it.

Those who seek Him in material things shall forever remain deluded...

The seer now makes a fervent appeal –

अजात इत्येवं कश्चिद्भीरुः प्रपद्यते ।
रुद्र यत्ते दक्षिणं मुखं तेन मां पाहि नित्यम् ॥४।२१॥

Some scared person (i.e., I, who am scared of death,) seeks refuge (in You) as the One who is unborn (Ajaata). O Rudra[9]! Please always protect me with that right profile of Yours.

This intriguing verse has several points of interest. The seeker has figured out that God is unborn. So, he is not looking for God in the visible Universe. Also, he is himself hoping to become 'Ajaata', i.e., achieve salvation.

Having accepted Him as invisible, it is weird to talk about His right profile! The weirdness is an indicator of a deeper meaning. The 'Daksha' in 'Dakshinam Mukham' (right profile) refers to expertise.[10] So, the prayer asks God to reveal His right profile – the teaching that will make us proficient in living life the way He wants. If we do not follow that advice, Rudra will come down heavily on us!

The seer, as if in ecstasy, ends the chapter with another prayer

9 Ref. verse 3|2.
10 That is why the right hand is called 'Dakshina Hasta' as it is more dexterous than the left one! The word 'dexterity' has itself arisen from 'Dakshataa'.

from the Vedas (Rg 10|114|8, Yajur 16|16) –

मा नस्तोके तनये मा न आयुषि
मा नो गोषु मा नो अश्वेषु रीरिषः ।
वीरान्मा नो रुद्र भामितो वधीर्-
हविष्मन्तः सदमित्त्वा हवामहे ॥४।२२॥

O Rudra! Please do not kill or harm our infants, or our children, or take away our years, or harm our cattle, or our beasts of burden and transport, or our valiant ones all fired up (against our enemies). Laden with offerings, we call you who are situated in justice (implying that, abiding by your laws, we perform Yajnas, i.e., sacrifices that protect the environment. There is a play on the word 'हवामहे' here which can mean both 'we call' and 'we perform Yajnas').

As with most Vaidika verses, the above verse can be read both as a prayer and as a teaching. While, on the one hand, it is a prayer to God as given above, on the other, for a young civilization, God preaches – your children, your animals and your armed forces are the wealth of your nation. Value them, protect them and multiply them.

Also, there is no other way but to accept God's laws (yes, He is a dictator!). Those who do accept and follow them become rich with wealth and happiness. One of these laws is that of giving back more to the environment than we take away. The Vedas preach that Yajnas are the best way of doing this. This is a non-obvious way. That is why the Vedas need to preach it. This science is largely undiscovered today.

❧

CHAPTER FIVE

Creation

❧

In this chapter, we find a detailed description of the creation of the Universe and the place of the Soul in it. It is surprising to find that this does not run counter to the scientific views held today. The chapter contains verses with great depth of meaning.

The seer, as is his wont, starts and ends the chapter with a description of God and His role –

द्वे अक्षरे ब्रह्मापरे त्वनन्ते
विद्याविद्ये निहिते यत्र गूढे ।
क्षरं त्वविद्या ह्यमृतं तु विद्या
विद्याविद्ये ईशते यस्तु सोऽन्यः ॥ ५। १॥

There are two indestructibles, other than Brahma, that are without an end (in time, not space), and in whom true knowledge (Vidyaa) and ignorance (Avidyaa) are situated in a concealed fashion. Ignorance is transient, while true knowledge is eternal. These two – Vidyaa and Avidyaa – are ruled over by yet Another (i.e.,God).

Here, in the first line, Vidyaa refers to the Soul, while Avidyaa refers to Matter, these being names based on their properties. Matter is regarded as lacking in Vidyaa, as it lacks intelligence. The Soul, on the other hand, is animate. So, it is capable of knowledge. God rules over both the animate and the inanimate worlds, determining what happens to them.

Vidyaa and Avidyaa have another meaning, too. That is why we again find a contradiction between the first and third lines of the verse – describing Avidyaa as immortal in the first and transient in the third. Avidyaa relates to knowledge about this transient material world, while Vidyaa relates to the unseen spiritual world. Avidyaa includes the delusion of living beings that they are their bodies and not something distinct from it. This knowledge is even more transient as the Soul occupies another body after death and then starts believing that the new body is its self now. This transient Avidyaa leads to more transience – entrapment in the cycle of birth and death, while knowledge of the trinity of immortals leads to immortality.

Again, we see a clear, unambiguous exposition of three immortal entities that are never created and are never destroyed.

Continuing from this verse, the seer says –

यो योनिं योनिमधितिष्ठत्येको
विश्वानि रूपाणि योनीश्च सर्वाः ।
ऋषिं प्रसूतं कपिलं यस्तमग्रे
ज्ञानैर्बिभर्ति जायमानं च पश्येत् ॥ ५।२ ॥

The One who single handedly presides over each and every cause (in this Universe), as also all the forms and species that exist, He is the One who creates the fiery (Kapila), changing (Rshi)[1] (Universe) in the beginning, nurtures it by His knowledge, and watches over it as it evolves.

---

1 *The words 'Rshi' and 'Kapila' have been interpreted by some as that God created the sage called Kapil in the beginning of the Universe and then watched over him, but this is absurd as humans cannot survive in the early Universe. Also, this is against traditional knowledge, which is given by Shwetaashwatara himself in 5|6.*

The word 'Yoni' in the first and second lines have different meanings. The first refers to primordial Matter, the ultimate cause, that gives rise to the many effects, i.e., all the objects in the Universe. The second Yoni refers to all the various life-forms that exist. The first meaning was encountered in 4|11, while the second one was found in 1|7, too.

'Kapila' means red or tawny. Here it implies the fiery early Universe, that was referred to earlier (3|4, 4|12) as Hiranyagarbha, or the golden womb. Both adjectives reflect the intense brightness of the early Universe.

'Rshi' has several meanings in Sanskrit, one of them being 'one that moves or changes'. This aptly describes the rapidly changing early Universe.

The word 'knowledge' here indicates that this Universe is an intelligent creation, and not a random one. This concept of an 'Intelligent Designer' is agreed to by an increasing number of scientists today, as against a probability-based Universe.

एकैकं जालं बहुधा विकुर्वन्-
नस्मिन् क्षेत्रे संहरत्येष देवः ।
भूयः सृष्ट्वा पतयस्तथेशः
सर्वाधिपत्यं कुरुते महात्मा ॥ ५। ३ ॥

This Divine Power diversifies each material interconnection into many types (e.g., the separation of the gravitational, etc., forces) in this field of the Universe, and also demolishes everything (completely at the time of Pralaya). Then, the Lord and Great Soul, having created the various lords (natural laws), presides over them.

It is remarkable that the word 'field' is used in English today to describe various 'forces at a distance'!

The verse describes the creation, destruction and then again creation in a never-ending cycle. It is also suggested that each time it is structurally the same as the last time. We should not be surprised by this because things that are perfect need no improvement!

The verse describes the creation of various lords of Nature. The Puranas embodied these forces of nature and made them animate. However, that is not how it is intended, neither here nor in the Vedas. Stories are always more popular than facts. So, the Puranic lore now has a stranglehold on Indian beliefs. This is the reason all the science in the Vedas is going abegging and Indians have become slaves to myths.

This description of the creation of the Universe tallies closely with some of the scientific theories today.

सर्वा दिश ऊर्ध्वमधश्च तिर्यक्
प्रकाशयन् भ्राजते यद्वनड्वान् ।
एवं स देवो भगवान् वरेण्यो
योनिस्वभावानधितिष्ठत्येकः ॥ ५।४ ॥

Just as the Sun, the giver of life, shines and lights up all the directions – above, below and the sides, so also that One Divinity, the Owner of all the wealth in the Universe, the One worth emulating, controls the nature of all the natural causes.

It is sought to make clear in this verse that the nature of things is 'natural' only because God has ordained them to be so. Some scientists feel it is unnecessary to have a God because everything functions according to its nature, without any external intervention. What they overlook is that that very nature has been established by God. The various symmetries of nature, and even more importantly, the asymmetries reflect but the beauty of the work of God.

Elaborating on the above theme, the seer says –

यच्च स्वभावं पचति विश्वयोनिः
पाच्यांश्च सर्वान् परिणामयेद्यः ।

सर्वमेतद् विश्वमधितिष्ठत्येको
गुणांश्च सर्वान् विनियोजयेद्यः ॥ ५। ५॥

He, the Cause of all causes, 'cooks' (develops to completion) the nature (of Matter), and then transforms all the cooked Matter (into the Universe). The One (Lord) controls everything in the Universe, and attaches everything to its properties.

As modern science avers, Matter undergoes a series of transformations after the Big Bang, which establishes all the primary particles and force fields. The interactions of these define the current Universe. This is exactly what this verse is also saying.

तद्वेदगुह्योपनिषत्सु गूढं
तद्ब्रह्मा वेदते ब्रह्मयोनिम् ।
ये पूर्वदेवा ऋषयश्च तद्विदुस्-
ते तन्मया अमृता वै बभूवुः ॥ ५। ६॥

That (above-described) Cause of the Universe and the Vedas, which is hidden in the teachings of the Vedas and the Upanishads is known by Brahmaa. Those early divine beings and sages who came to know It, they became full of Him and (thus) definitely achieved immortality.

As per our tradition, Brahmaa (as distinct from the neuter gender word 'Brahma' used for God) is the name of the sage who first imbibed all the four Vedas. He, thus, understood the full cause-and-effect matrix of this Universe down to the ultimate Cause, i.e., Brahma. All those who followed in his footsteps achieved the same fate – salvation from reincarnation.

Switching focus to the Jeeva (living being), the seer details its nature –

गुणान्वयो यः फलकर्मकर्ता
कृतस्य तस्यैव स चोपभोक्ता ।

स विश्वरूपस्त्रिगुणस्त्रिवर्त्मा
प्राणाधिपः सञ्चरति स्वकर्मभिः ॥ ५।७॥

The one who is enveloped by the qualities (Gunas, i.e., Sattva, Raja and Tama of Matter, that makes up his body) and does deeds in order to obtain some gratification or the other, he is also the consumer of (the results of) those deeds. He takes on all the different forms (of the various bodies that he occupies); he has three properties (Gunas, as above); he treads on three paths. Depending on his deeds, this Ruler of Praana (life-force) roams (these three paths).

In a very concise form, the seer has given all details of life and living. The independence in performing action, and the dependence (on God) in getting its rewards, is clearly laid down here. While the Soul decides what action to take based on the expected reward, its attachment to the reward ensures that it continues to shuttle between different bodies. These various forms are its 'Vishwaroopa'.

Matter has the three properties of Sattva, Raja and Tama in equal proportion at the beginning of Creation. It gets differentiated into different types of objects when this equality is disturbed. These same properties are found in varying proportions in living bodies, too, and determine the nature of the living being. Saattvika individuals are pure, benevolent, happy and devoted to studies related to Dharma and spirituality. Raajasika individuals are given to action, material desires, valour and sadness. Taamasika individuals are lazy, greedy, cruel and ignorant.[2] Humans have the unique capability in the living world of being able to alter their nature by self-control, type of food intake, type of activities undertaken, etc.

The three paths refer to the path of evolved beings (Devayaana), the path of humans (Pitryaana) and the path of other species (Tiryaka-yoni). Immersing oneself in God leads to divinity and immortality. Living a relatively ethical life, with some righteous

---

2 *Ref. Manusmrti, Chapter 12, and Bhagawad Gitaa, Chapter 14, for more details.*

deeds and some not so much, and with actions based on desire – in short, leading an ethical materialistic life – leads to a human birth. Evil deeds lead to demotion to other forms of life.

Calling the Soul a Ruler of Praana brings out the fact that, not only is the Soul the cause of life in the body, but that we also have some control on the duration of our life and that of our species, even though the ultimate control resides with the Supreme. Thus, beings give birth to offspring by their actions, and control the extent of their own lives to a limited extent, e.g., regular physical activity can increase the lifespan, while standing in front of an oncoming truck can shorten it!

Continuing the description of the Soul, the sage says –

अङ्गुष्ठमात्रो रवितुल्यरूपः
सङ्कल्पाहङ्कारसमन्वितो यः ।
बुद्धेर्गुणेनात्मगुणेन चैव
आराग्रमात्रो ह्यपरोऽपि दृष्टः ॥ ५।८ ॥

The other (the Soul that is other than God) is seen (by the meditator) by means of the qualities of the intellect and by his own qualities (Saatvika properties, to be precise). (He sees the Soul as possessing the following qualities –) He is the size of a thumb or the point of a needle, has the brilliance of the Sun, is enveloped by the desire to take action (Sankalpa) and perception of unity with the body (Ahankaara).

In 3|13, God was described as the size of the thumb. Here, the Soul is defined as such. In the same breath, it is called as something much smaller than even the thumb – the size of the point of a needle. All this goes to indicate that these words are not to be taken literally. The seer just implies that the Soul is extremely subtle and cannot be measured in terms of material objects. Only an idea can be given of them by material analogies. Also, as explained in 3|13, the seeker must meditate on the thumb-sized region of the brain for this revelation.

The Soul is as radiant as the Sun, because, of its own, it is devoid of ignorance and faults. It is only when it is placed in the body that it is enveloped by Sankalpa and Ahankaara. These are material qualities, but seem to get transplanted onto the Soul in its own perception.

Again, we see the method of meditation, given earlier in Chapter 2, incorporates using the intellect to first connect with one's true Self, and then, using the Self to connect with God.

Further describing the Soul, the seer says –

वालाग्रशतभागस्य शतधा कल्पितस्य च ।
भागो जीवः स विज्ञेयः स चानन्त्याय कल्पते ॥ ५।९॥

When the hundredth part of the tip of the hair is further split a hundred times, then one should know that one part as the size of the Soul. This Soul is without an end (in time, i.e., it never dies).

We see the sage giving another size for the Soul here. All these are just to drive home the point that the Soul is much subtler than the body.

It is an axiom in Indian philosophy that what has no beginning can have no end, and, contrariwise, that which has a beginning must have an end. Thus, the seer is implying that the Soul, too, is without beginning or end, which in turn implies that it is never created or destroyed.

As if explaining the Vaidika verse given in 4|3, the sage says –

नैव स्त्री न पुमानेष न चैवायं नपुंसकः ।
यद्यच्छरीरमादत्ते तेन तेन स युज्यते ॥ ५।१०॥

The Soul is neither a woman, nor a man, nor is it a eunuch. Whatever body it accepts, it unites with that (to acquire its gender and, by extension, all its other physical and mental attributes).

This should encourage us to be kind and humane to all beings and to not have class or gender distinctions. Who knows, we may tomorrow be the being we are insulting today!

Of course, the body the Soul does get is a complex result of the deeds it has performed in previous births. This is explained in the next verse –

सङ्कल्पनस्पर्शनदृष्टिमोहैर्-
ग्रासाम्बुवृष्ट्या चात्मविवृद्धिजन्म ।
कर्मानुगान्यनुक्रमेण देही
स्थानेषु रूपाण्यभिसम्प्रपद्यते ॥ ५। १९ ॥

The embodied Soul attains the determination to perform actions (Sankalpana), the senses including those of touch (Sparshana) and vision (Drshti), as also the delusion of being the body it occupies (Moha). This Self grows and is born through food, water and insemination. According to its deeds or as per a specified sequence, it acquires different forms in different locations.

Only when the Soul is deluded into thinking that it is the body will it work towards protecting it, nourishing it, reproducing it. This is the delusion that the seeker has to work against.

In the animal kingdom, there is no freedom of action. So, the Soul does not acquire any Phala for its instinctive actions as an animal. Whatever it suffers or enjoys during its life is determined by its deeds in previous births as a human being. Thus, the next birth of the Soul which is not in a human form is determined more by the hierarchy of living things than its deeds, moving up the hierarchy one birth at a time. This is what is meant by Anukramena – in a specified sequence. It is only in the human birth that we can act according to our wish, and break that order. We can rise to Moksha or fall down to plant level. To avoid the latter eventuality, it is important for us to understand Dharma, the eternal path for happiness and spiritual progress.

While 'forms' refers to the different species, 'location' refers to not only geographical or planetary location, but also one's status in life – whether one is born in a high-class or a poor family, whether an intellectual or an illiterate family. This determines the quantum of happiness and sorrow that one encounters in life.

Elaborating further, the seer says –

स्थूलानि सूक्ष्माणि बहूनि चैव
रूपाणि देही स्वगुणैर्वृणोति।
क्रियागुणैरात्मगुणैश्च तेषां
संयोगहेतुरपरोऽपि दृष्टः ॥५।१२॥

Based on its qualities, the embodied Soul acquires many microscopic and macroscopic forms. These qualities can be classified as those of its deeds and those of itself (i.e., of its mind, viz fairness, gentleness, wickedness, cruelty, etc.).[3] These form the basis for its next birth. However, a cause other than these has also been seen (by the seers in their meditation[4]).

This latter cause, of course, is God who finally determines who goes where, applying a complex algorithm and His own judgement.

Clarifying this cause, Shwetaashwatara exults into an eulogy of God in the last two verses, beginning with almost a repetition of verse 4|11 –

अनाद्यन्तं कलिलस्य मध्ये
विश्वस्य स्रष्टारमनेकरूपम्।

3 'Aatmaguna' is usually interpreted as 'the Soul's own qualities'. However, the qualities that bind the Soul to the body are those of its material body and not its own, as explained in earlier verses. If it was its own qualities that entrapped it in its body, then it would never be able to achieve salvation, as it would not be able to modify that quality.
4 Ref. verse 1|3

विश्वस्यैकं परिवेष्टितारं
ज्ञात्वा देवं मुच्यते सर्वपाशैः ॥५।१३॥

In this (seemingly) chaotic Universe, there is One without a beginning or an end, who is the Creator of everything, takes on many forms (as if of all the inanimate forms in the Universe), and envelops all. Knowing this Divine Being, the Soul is released of all bonds.

भावग्राह्यमनीडाख्यं भावाभावकरं शिवम् ।
कलासर्गकरं देवं ये विदुस्ते जहुस्तनुम् ॥५।१४॥

This Shiva – the Auspicious Divine Being – is to be grasped by meditation and devotion. He is called the One without a support. He is the Creator and the Destroyer. He is also the One who creates the elements (Kalaas) of Creation (sixteen of them, as described in 1/4). Those who know Him give up their bodies (i.e., their bondage with Matter).

Without achieving discernment between Matter, the Soul and the Supreme, salvation from this cycle of life and death is out of question.

❧

CHAPTER SIX

The Questions Answered, Surrender Ensues

❧

This chapter ends the Upanishad with the answer to the questions that were framed in the very first verse, bringing to an end the quest for truth that it had started out with. Having traversed the length and breadth of Creation, it ends with complete surrender and ultimate devotion to its Creator – the Supreme, going into ecstasies in describing His nature and actions. The whole chapter is worth memorising!

स्वभावमेके कवयो वदन्ति
कालं तथान्ये परिमुह्यमानाः ।
देवस्यैष महिमा तु लोके
येनेदं भ्राम्यते ब्रह्मचक्रम् ॥ ६। १॥

Some learned ones say that this Universe is created by its very Nature; others say Time is the cause; but, they are both deluded. (In reality,) it is the Lord's greatness in this world which causes the Wheel of the Universe to rotate.

Very perceptively, the seer calls even the deluded ones 'the learned ones'! Even today, we find it is the scientists who have the most doubts about the existence of God, while the common person accepts it easily. Too much rationalising can sometimes take one away from the obvious, or that which requires a belief in a higher authority!

Elaborating on the thought, the sage says –

येनावृतं नित्यमिदं हि सर्वं
ज्ञः कालकालो गुणी सर्वविद्यः ।
तेनेशितं कर्म विवर्तते ह
पृथ्व्यप्तेजोऽनिलखानि चिन्त्यम् ॥ ६। २॥

He by whom everything is perpetually enveloped, He who is the Embodiment of knowledge, the Time of time, or the Death of death (i.e., controls time and death), who (even though He is devoid of all qualities created by Matter) has many qualities (like consciousness, impartiality, kindness, blissfulness, etc.), and who is Omniscient, the action that is controlled by Him exists in diverse forms - Earth, Liquid, Heat, Gas and Space (the five elements). (This is how the cause of the Universe) should be pondered over.

Generically, 'Kaala' refers to time. However, death being a function of time, it is also referred to as 'Kaala', as can also be found in the English phrase, 'His time had come'. The One who controls either of these is then the Time of time and the Death of death!

Typically, the word 'Guna' (quality) is associated with the properties of Matter in philosophical texts. However, every once in a while, it also refers to the qualities intrinsic to the two spirits – God and the Soul. In this verse, the qualities of God are being referred to when God is called 'the One with qualities (Gunee)'.

The Universe, with all its paraphernalia, is referred to as the 'action of God' here. It is an intelligent Creation and could not have been created randomly – this should be comprehended by the seeker of truth. Otherwise little progress can be made towards the ultimate goal.

तत्कर्म कृत्वा विनिवर्त्य भूयस्-
तत्त्वस्य तत्त्वेन समेत्य योगम् ।
एकेन द्वाभ्यां त्रिभिरष्टभिर्वा
कालेन चैवात्मगुणैश्च सूक्ष्मैः ॥ ६।३॥

Many times He performs this deed, and many times He finishes it (in the form of Pralaya) (i.e., there are many creations of the Universe ending in dissolutions). (During creation,) He joins one entity (the Soul) with another entity (Matter). Alternatively, (the Soul may be considered as) conjoined to One (=ignorance), or Two (=good and bad deeds), or three (the three gunas of Sattva, Raja and Tama), or eight (= the five elements, Mana, Ahankaara and Buddhi),[1] as well as Time, and the subtle (mental) properties of the Soul (goodness, kindness, evil, etc.).

Again, the repetition of the cycle of creation and dissolution of the Universe is emphasised. The verse also hints at it being the same in form and substance in each cycle. That is why the terms – time, the five elements, etc. – valid for this Universe, are also sufficient to describe all the past universes and those yet to come.

The next three verses further explain that the Universe revolves because of and for the Souls. Their deeds form the primary cause of Creation. These verses should be read together.

आरभ्य कर्माणि गुणान्वितानि
भावांश्च सर्वान् विनियोजयेद्यः ।
तेषामभावे कृतकर्मनाशः
कर्मक्षये याति स तत्त्वतोऽन्यः ॥ ६।४॥

---

1 Ref. verse 2|1.

When the one (Soul), performing deeds that have Gunas (Sattva, Raja, Tama), sublimates all his desires (into God), then in the absence of desires, (the fruits of) his earlier deeds are destroyed. With his deeds destroyed, the Soul moves as one who is different from the other (i.e., Matter).

The Soul performs deeds only in association with a body. By itself it is incapable of action. Thus, ultimately, the deeds are performed by a body that is composed of Matter that, in turn, has three basic properties – Sattva, Raja and Tama. That is why the deeds are said to have these three properties, too.

There are two types of deeds – Sakaama Karma and Nishkaama Karma. The first is the product of desires for material pleasures. Therefore, it is indulged in by lesser mortals. Take away this desire for the material, and what is left is the latter type of Karma. Nishkaama Karma is performed by higher mortals and God. The Universe is such a deed of God. He creates it for the Souls, and has nothing to gain Himself from it. Therefore, none of His actions has any impact on His being. It does not bear fruit in the form of happiness and sorrow for Him. For the Soul to attain this state, it must make the desire for God the over-arching desire. The moment personal desires are missing from the action of a Soul, Matter gives up its grip on the Soul and the Soul is free to be itself.

It is worth noting that neither God, nor the Soul, can really perform actions for themselves or on themselves. They perform them on Matter, and their effect involves modifying Matter alone.

आदिः स संयोगनिमित्तहेतुः
परस्त्रिकालादकलोऽपि दृष्टः ।
तं विश्वरूपं भवभूतमीड्यं
देवं स्वचित्तस्थमुपास्य पूर्वम् ॥ ६।५॥

He (God) is the Beginning. He is the efficient cause[2] of the union (of the Soul with Matter). He is beyond the three times (past, present and future). He is also seen without Kalaas. The Soul should first meditate upon this Divine Being as the One who takes on all forms (of the Universe), reveals Himself as the Universe (so to speak), worthy of adoration and situated inside one's intellect.

God has been called the Beginning because He is the One who becomes active first at the time of Creation. He 'awakens' the sleeping Souls and Matter, so to speak. He is, thus, the Cause for the rest of the Universe, but is Himself without a cause!

Being the efficient cause, the seer implies that God does not form part of either the Soul or Matter; He is only responsible for bringing them together so that they can unite. The Soul and Matter form material causes of a living being.

Earlier, we had seen that God has sixteen Kalaas[3]. These Kalaas are actually the characteristics of the Universe created by Him. The verse is telling us that He is not bound by the Universe, and exists beyond and apart from it, too. This has to be so, because if the Universe is expanding, and God never changes in his characteristics, then the Universe must expand *into* Him – He must already exist outside it.[4]

In the usual enigmatic style of yore, having just described God as having all the forms of the Universe, the seer now says its opposite –

स वृक्षकालाकृतिभिः परोऽन्यो
यस्मात् प्रपञ्चः परिवर्ततेऽयम् ।
धर्मावहं पापनुदं भगेशं
ज्ञात्वात्मस्थममृतं विश्वधाम ॥ ६ । ६ ॥

---

2 Ref. Introduction, point 7.
3 Ref. verse 1|4.
4 Ref. verse 3|20.

He (God) is distinct from the tree (of the Universe, as described in verses 4|6-7), Time and Form. It is because of Him that this world keeps moving. Knowing Him (thus and) as the One who encourages Dharma and discourages Sin, who is the Lord of all the wealth, who is located inside the seeker's very self, who is devoid of Death (i.e., going from existence to non-existence) and is the support of everything, (the seeker gets disassociated from Matter).[5]

Thus, the above three verses together say that, to see God, one must first meditate upon Him (6|5), and then come to realise Him (6|6), upon which his deeds will become Nishkaama and he will achieve salvation (6|4). The meditation may start by visualising the Universe as the body of God (6|5), but the ultimate realisation is to see His true existence as a Being without form (6|6) and with all the qualities that the verses are declaring repeatedly. The seer then starts seeing God behind each and every movement of the Universe. Upon enlightenment, the Soul becomes devoid of Karma and moves independent of Matter. While the body will continue to cling to the seer till the end of this life, she will now know it to be separate from her true self.

The one who has glimpsed God now breaks forth in ecstasy –

तमीश्वराणां परमं महेश्वरं
तं देवतानां परमं च दैवतम् ।
पतिं पतीनां परमं परस्ताद्-
विदाम देवं भुवनेशमीड्यम् ॥ ६ । ७ ॥

He is the Lord of lords, the Great Lord. He is the most Divine of all the divinities. He is the Controller of controllers, and far beyond everything. We have come to know that adorable Divine Being, who is the Lord of the world.

'Eeshwaras' here does not mean many Gods, but rather the

---

5 *This part of the sentence is taken from verse 6|4 as the three verses together make one sentence.*

owners of wealth or of good qualities. Similarly, 'Devataas' refers to the divine natural forces. 'Patis' refers to the various controllers in Nature or among human beings.

The rest of the Upanishad continues in the same vein and is essentially an eulogy of God sung by somebody who is overcome with emotion on seeing the Divine. These beautiful verses are worth including in one's prayer routine.

In the following famous verse, the sage says –

न तस्य कार्यं करणं च विद्यते
न तत्समश्चाभ्यधिकश्च दृश्यते ।
परास्य शक्तिर्विविधैव श्रूयते
स्वाभाविकी ज्ञानबलक्रिया च ॥ ६।८ ॥

There exists no effect or instrument of this Being (i.e., He is not transformed into anything else, nor does He require any instrument in order to perform His tasks). There is none seen equal to Him, nor greater. It is said that His power is beyond anybody else's and is multifarious. Knowledge, strength and action are natural to Him (He does not have to develop them, or take assistance from anyone or anything).

It is foolish to think that He transforms into any material object (an effect), even if it is animate, as in a human Avataara. The Creator of the Universe does not need to take up a body to either perform any task, or give any teaching. His teachings are available through the Vedas and seers.

He also does not have any instrument to help Him to create the world, for if He needed some instrument, that instrument may be considered as powerful as Him, like the concept of the various Devas in the Puraanas, who keep fighting with each other. But this is not true. His powers exceed anybody else's by a huge margin. Also, they are extremely varied – He creates the smallest of atoms and the largest of galaxies, and everything in between.

The knowledge, the power and the actions required to create and run the Universe, are all inherent in Him – nothing or nobody gives it to Him. He operates alone.

न तस्य कश्चित् पतिरस्ति लोके
न चेशिता नैव च तस्य लिङ्गम्।
स कारणं करणाधिपाधिपो
न चास्य कश्चिज्जनिता न चाधिपः ॥ ६।९॥

There is no controller of Him in this world, nor a lord above Him, nor does He have any identification mark (there is nothing you can perceive and say, "Look, that is God!"). He is the (ultimate) Cause, the Lord of the lords of the instruments. No one, or nothing, gave birth to Him, nor does He have a ruler above Him.

Typically, the senses are seen as instruments, particularly as they include both the senses of perception and action. The lord of these instruments is the Soul. Then, the Lord of the lord of instruments means God, i.e., God who is the Lord of all Souls.

If any of the statements in the verse was not true, it would imply that somebody or something was capable of interfering with the functioning of God. For example, if something was required to give birth to Him at the beginning of the Universe, that thing would become more important and powerful than God Himself. For this reason, He is, and shall remain for all eternity, the Cause of all causes – the ultimate Cause.

यस्तन्तुनाभ इव तन्तुभिः प्रधानजैः स्वभावतो देव एकः स्वमावृणोत्।
स नो दधाद्ब्रह्माप्ययम् ॥ ६।१०॥

Just like a spider covers itself with the threads of the web, the One Divinity, by His very nature, covers Himself with the transformations of primordial Matter (i.e., the Universe). May this Lord give us entry into Brahma, i.e., Himself!

The connotation is that Brahma is extremely well hidden in the Universe. To uncover Him, we need to look beyond Matter. Also, and* more importantly, we need His Grace to see Him.

Sometimes we wonder – why did this Universe have to be created at all? Why did the Souls have to be given a body in which they experience so much grief? The answer is simple – that is the nature of things. All questioning must end at a truth, whether it is a self-evident axiom or not. Beyond that, it is meaningless to ask questions. The Souls must connect with Matter, and live a life in which they experience joys and sorrows. They must grow internally and overcome their shortcomings, till they are finally ready to see the Divine.

एको देवः सर्वभूतेषु गूढः
सर्वव्यापी सर्वभूतान्तरात्मा ।
कर्माध्यक्षः सर्वभूताधिवासः
साक्षी चेता केवलो निर्गुणश्च ॥ ६।११॥

That One Divinity is hidden in all created things. He is Omnipresent and the Soul of all Souls. He presides over the (consequences of) deeds. He resides above everything (i.e., they are controlled by Him). He is a Witness (to all actions), is Ever-conscious, is complete in Himself and devoid of all properties imposed by Matter.

'Karmaadhyaksha' should not be understood as the One who controls all deeds per se. The Soul is free to decide its actions. Instead, the word implies that God determines the results of those actions.

A number of these characteristics are also shared by the Soul, but sometimes to a limited extent. For example, the Soul is also conscious, but not always. During sleep, it becomes unconscious, as also at the time of Pralaya (dissolution). Similarly, the Soul is hidden inside the body, controls its actions, controls Matter to a limited extent, is an observer inside the body, is untouched by Matter at the deepest level.

एको वशी निष्क्रियाणां बहूना-
मेकं बीजं बहुधा यः करोति ।
तमात्मस्थं येऽनुपश्यन्ति धीरास्-
तेषां सुखं शाश्वतं नेतरेषाम् ॥ ६। १२॥[6]

The One is the Controller of many (read 'all') inanimate objects, and is the One who makes manifold the one seed (of primordial Matter). Those steadfast seers who see Him situated inside their souls, for them there is eternal happiness, and for no other.

Primordial Matter starts out as a single uniform entity – the seed of the Universe. God splits it into all the diverse objects we see today. This is possible because He has complete control of Matter. The individual Soul also has some control in shaping things, but that is very limited indeed.

The seer has to be steadfast in order to continue on the extremely difficult path of the discovery of God. As Kathopanishad 1|3|14 declares – क्षुरस्य धारा निशिता दुरत्यया दुर्गं पथस्तत् कवयो वदन्ति – the wise ones say that the road to immortality is as tough to tread as walking on a razor's edge, an edge that has been sharpened to a point.

Also, the seer notes that to see God, one has to look within and not without.

Again, he repeats that seeing your true self and Him is the only path to salvation; there is no other.

---

6 *This verse is similar to Kathopanishad 2|2|12.*

नित्यो नित्यानां चेतनश्चेतनाना-
  मेको बहूनां यो विदधाति कामान् ।
तत्कारणं साङ्ख्ययोगाधिगम्यं
  ज्ञात्वा देवं मुच्यते सर्वपाशैः ॥ ६। १३ ॥[7]

He is the Eternal of the eternals and the Animate of the animates.
He is the One who fulfils the desires of many (i.e., all the living beings).
Knowing that Divine Being, who is the (Efficient) Cause (of the Universe)
and is to be known through the disciplines of Sankhya and Yoga, one
is released of all fetters.

There are six ancient systems of Indian philosophy, viz Saankhya, Yoga, Nyaaya, Vaisheshika, Poorva- and Uttara-meemaansa. Of these, Saankhya deals with knowledge regarding the material Universe, while Yoga deals with the spiritual Universe, i.e., it describes how to attain union with God through righteousness, renunciation and meditation. Thus, we note again, as we did earlier in 4|17, that ancient seers considered knowledge of the Universe to be as critical to understanding Brahma as direct knowledge of Him through meditation. Interestingly, the stated goal of Saankhya is to attain Moksha, too. Those who lay great emphasis on Bhakti-yoga, to the exclusion of right knowledge, are the ones to get deluded by things like representations of God in mud, or belief in music being the path to God, or of the efficacy of meditation without first purifying one's actions, etc. To be able to figure out fact from fiction, one has to be well educated. Just as an illiterate person may think that the Earth is flat, an ignorant spiritual person may believe a material object represents God. The spiritual seeker has to know where Matter ends and the Spirit begins.

---

7 *This verse is similar to Kathopanishad 2|2|13.*

न तत्र सूर्यो भाति न चन्द्रतारकं
नेमा विद्युतो भान्ति कुतोऽयमग्निः ।
तमेव भान्तमनुभाति सर्वं
तस्य भासा सर्वमिदं विभाति ॥ ६। १४॥[8]

The Sun does not shine there, nor the moon, nor the stars, nor does lightening, what to speak of this fire! (That is, their brilliance pales in comparison to His light.) That light (of God) is radiated by all (other luminous) bodies. His brilliance lights up everything else.

As we saw earlier, God is very often referred to as intense light.[9] A number of Vaidika mantras describe Him the same way. It is possible that this is how God appears to the enlightened Soul.

एको हँसो भुवनस्यास्य मध्ये
स एवाग्निः सलिले सन्निविष्टः ।
तमेव विदित्वाति मृत्युमेति
नान्यः पन्था विद्यतेऽयनाय[10] ॥ ६। १५॥

That One Mover[11] exists in the middle of this Universe. He alone is the Fire that is inherent in the ocean (of subtle matter). Knowing Him alone does one go beyond death. There exists no other path to immortality.

'Agni' is another Vaidika word that has many meanings. Here, it refers to the energy that exists in all of Matter. While there is energy in all matter by itself, God is the Energy of that energy!

The Vedas and the seers do not tire of telling us that there is only one very narrow path to salvation, but those who do not know this path many a times take it upon themselves to mislead their devotees

---

8 *This verse is also found in Kathopanishad 2|2|15 and Mundakopanishad 2|2|10.*
9 *Ref. verse 3|8.*
10. *The last two lines of the verse are the same as 3|8 and Yajurveda 31|18.*
11 *See verse 3|18.*

by telling them that all paths ultimately lead to Him!! Nothing could be farther from the truth.

The seer starts summarising the answer to the question that was posed at the beginning of the Upanishad –

स विश्वकृद्विश्वविदात्मयोनिर्-
ज्ञः कालकालो गुणी सर्वविद्यः[12] ।
प्रधानक्षेत्रज्ञपतिर्गुणेशः
संसारमोक्षस्थितिबन्धहेतुः ॥ ६। १६॥

He is the Creator of all, the Knower of all that goes on, His own Cause. He, who is the Embodiment of knowledge, the Time of time or the Death of death,[13] the Possessor of all good qualities, the Knower of everything, is the Lord of the Soul – the one who knows the field of Matter (the Universe), the Controller of all material properties, the Cause of the bondage, maintenance and release (of the Soul in a material body) in this world.

While the Universe and life have efficient, material and general causes,[14] God has none of them. He is the Causeless Cause. Nobody or nothing else has any role in what He is for the simple reason that He does not transform into anything. This again emphasises the fact that Matter cannot influence Him, let alone envelop Him in a human or any other form.

'Pradhaana' is the word used for primordial Matter. Its 'Kshetra', or field, is the Universe (Pradhaanakshetra). The knower of this field is the Soul (Pradhaanakshetrajna), i.e., the Soul has the capability to understand the physics, chemistry and biology of the Universe. The Lord of this knower is Brahma (Pradhaanakshetrajnapati). As with the word 'Karanaadhipaadhipa' in verse 6|9, we see multiple compounding of words in this word. The same is present in the word

---

12 *This line is the same as verse 6|2.*
13 *See verse 6|2.*
14 *Ref. Introduction, point 7.*

'Sansaaramokshasthitibandhahetu'. This abbreviation process is a unique and beautiful feature of the Sanskrit language.

God is 'Gunesha', the One who controls the properties of nature. Thus, a tsunami may seem to occur due to very scientific reasons, however complex those reasons may appear to us. But in the ultimate analysis, He set the events in motion which lead to it eons ago!

The first verse had asked who is the great cause of the Universe, from where living beings had come, where they were established and who was meting out happiness and sorrow to them. All questions get answered explicitly in this verse – God is the Cause of the Universe, bringing together Matter and Souls to create living beings, establishing them in their proper places here and ruling over them all. He alone determines the birth of a Soul, maintains it in life, and releases it in death, or salvation.

The seer continues to elaborate the answer to these questions –

स तन्मयो ह्यमृत ईशसंस्थो
ज्ञः सर्वगो भुवनस्यास्य गोप्ता।
य ईशे अस्य जगतो नित्यमेव
नान्यो हेतुर्विद्यत ईशनाय ॥ ६। १७॥

He is full of Himself alone (is not corrupted by anything else), is Immortal and resides within the controllers of the natural world. He is the Embodiment of knowledge, has gone everywhere (is Omnipresent) and is the Protector of the habitable worlds. There exists no other cause for ruling this Universe, than He who rules over this world at all times.

Having laid down the principles behind the Universe, the seer surrenders totally to its Cause –

यो ब्रह्माणं विदधाति पूर्वं
यो वै वेदांश्च प्रहिणोति तस्मै।

तं ह देवमात्मबुद्धिप्रकाशं
मुमुक्षुर्वै शरणमहं प्रपद्ये ॥ ६। १८ ॥

The One who created Brahmaa in the beginning (early days of humanity), the One who surely revealed the Vedas to him, I, who am desirous of attaining salvation (Mumukshu), take refuge in that Divine Being who generates knowledge of Himself.

Thus, again it is clarified that Vedas are the word of God. He gave them to mankind to make known the difference between righteousness and wrongdoing – Dharma and Adharma.

God cannot be known without His own grace. The seeker has to submit herself to Him with complete devotion.

Continuing the description of God from the previous verse, the seer says –

निष्कलं निष्क्रियं शान्तं निरवद्यं निरञ्जनम् ।
अमृतस्य परं सेतुं दग्धेन्धनमिवानलम् ॥ ६। १९ ॥

God is without parts, without motion (Nishkriya), is tranquil, devoid of the unspeakable (i.e., faults), devoid of impurities, the ultimate bridge for attaining immortality (for crossing the tempestuous waters of this world), and like a fire whose fuel has been burnt (i.e., does not contain remnants of the fuel like smoke, soot, etc., but is pure energy and light).

Nishkriya can also be interpreted as performing no action, in the sense mentioned in 3|20 and 6|4.

The seer now makes a resounding declaration –

यदा चर्मवदाकाशं वेष्टयिष्यन्ति मानवाः ।
तदा देवमविज्ञाय दुःखस्यान्तो भविष्यति ॥ ६। २० ॥

The day that humans (are able to) wrap the sky in a skin, that will be the day when sorrow (for the Soul) will end without knowing the Lord.

The seer rhetorically means that this will never happen. Seeing God is the only door to release one from bondage.

Bringing the Upanishad to a close, the initial discussion is referred to where the Brahmavaadis had gone into meditation to understand the cause of the Universe (verse 1|3). Shwetaashwatara was one of those. The Upanishad has been written by one of his disciples to record the words of the seer. This slice of history is revealed in this verse –

तपःप्रभावाद्देवप्रसादाच्च ब्रह्म
ह श्वेताश्वतरोऽथ विद्वान् ।
अत्याश्रमिभ्यः परमं पवित्रं
प्रोवाच सम्यगृषिसङ्घजुष्टम् ॥ ६।२१॥

By the impact of the austerities performed, and by the grace of God, Shwetaashwatara came to know Brahma. He, who receives devotion from the community of sages (Rshis), then preached about the Ultimate and Pure (Brahma, or the ultimately Pure Brahma) to those who have gone beyond Aashramas[15] (i.e., the Sanyaasis who are in search of God).

Giving a word of caution to the guru who plans to teach about Brahma, the disciple says –

वेदान्ते परमं गुह्यं पुराकल्पे प्रचोदितम् ।
नाप्रशान्ताय दातव्यं नापुत्रायाशिष्याय वा पुनः ॥ ६।२२॥

The above-mentioned teaching about Brahma, which is the most secret part covered in the end of the Vedas and has been transmitted since ancient times, should not be handed down to those who are not one's students or offspring or are not tranquil in mind.

This kind of warning has been given in other Upanishads as well. It seems strange that any restriction should be placed on such a beneficial sermon. Also, if the student is already tranquil in mind,

---

15 *Ref. verse 4|9*

does s/he really need the teaching? This paradox can be understood as follows. It is the guru's duty to transmit the knowledge to his/her children. Also, the guru should acquire students, in case s/he already does not have some, and transmit his learning. This son/daughter or student may not be tranquil in mind, since the guru has yet to show them the way. However, the seeker must be assured that the guru knows what he is talking about. This in itself requires a belief that such a teaching exists and is good for oneself. To that extent, the student is already primed for this teaching, which has very little visible proof to support it. On the other hand, if the knowledge is given to a 'casual' student, a rank outsider, the guru will face a big hurdle in first overcoming the doubts about his own self-worth. Also, the listener may only ridicule the knowledge being transmitted and, worse still, turn away from the subject itself.

This is further detailed in the next verse, the last verse of the Upanishad, that describes the ideal student –

यस्य देवे परा भक्तिर्यथा देवे तथा गुरौ।
तस्यैते कथिता ह्यर्थाः प्रकाशन्ते महात्मनः ।
प्रकाशन्ते महात्मनः ॥ ६ । २ ३ ॥

The (student) who has the ultimate devotion for God and, as for God, so for the guru, the meanings of the teachings definitely illuminate themselves to this great Soul.

Unthinking, unquestioning faith is not what is meant here. When we do not understand the purport of some teachings, we should not hesitate to ask the guru. In fact, questions indicate that the student is mulling over the material taught. However, what is being spoken about here is the confidence that the student should have that the guru knows the answers. If there is doubt in the enlightenment of the guru, there is nothing that the student will ever gain. So, the student should also seek out a teacher whose learning s/he respects, and then imbibe the knowledge with full devotion.

Uttara Nerurkar is a B.Tech. in Chemical Engineering from the Indian Institute of Technology, Kanpur. She worked for 15 years in leading chemical engineering and software companies, her last stint being as a Software Researcher at Infosys Limited, where she served for over eight years. As a researcher, she co-authored a book on software engineering for Tata McGraw Hill. Her research papers have been published in international software magazines and journals, such as Dr. Dobb's Journal and IEEE Software Journal, and presented at international conferences.

Since 2001, Uttara has been pursuing the path of Adhyaatma and studying the Vedas, Upanishads, Darshan Shastras and other Indian philosophical treatises, along with Sanskrit. She has studied at the feet of Swami Brahmadevaji, Smt. Amrutvarshini Bhatt, Acharya Anandprakash, Acharya Satyananda Vedvageesh, Smt. Pushpa Dixit and many other gurus of different schools of thought. Her intensive studies have been recognised by experts. She presented a paper on *Nyayadarshanam,* the ancient Indian text on Logic and reasoning, at the prestigious 16th World Sanskrit Conference, Bangkok, 2015. Another of her papers on the same text was published in India's foremost philosophical journal – Journal of the Indian Council of Philosophical Research. She has presented her studies on other ancient Indian philosophical texts in many other national and international conferences. She regularly writes in renowned Vaidika magazines like *Dayanand Sandesh, Vedavaani,* etc., and gives discourses on Vaidika subjects in various community forums. She has been teaching the Upanishads, Manusmrti, Bhagawad-geeta, etc., as also Sanskrit, for the past ten years.

She strongly believes that the knowledge that is contained in our ancient texts is extremely relevant today. She has been trying to spread this message by giving presentations to schools and colleges, speaking at various national and international conferences, and producing videos in English, Hindi and Tamil that are freely available on YouTube. Her message is to echo the clarion call of Swami Dayanand Saraswati of the Arya Samaja – 'Go back to the Vedas.'

Website: http://indianvedas.net/

YouTube: https://www.youtube.com/user/Nerurkar150

Audio of Lectures, e.g., Bhagawad-geeta - https://drive.google.com/ drive/#folders/0B-f6xL6_iU7TalRLZkhOWkFWME0

www.ingramcontent.com/pod-product-compliance
Lightning Source LLC
LaVergne TN
LVHW051809080426

835513LV00017B/1876